Uncle Dick,
We are so
honored that you
married us! Thank you so
much for your love, time, a
travel. This is our favorite
book of Colorado and wanted to
share it.

Love,
Sara + Charlie

MW01013492

Colorado:
Yesterday & Today

Joseph Collier  Grant Collier

Grant Collier

Collier Publishing

Lakewood, CO

Printed in Canada

ISBN 0-9769218-0-4
Text design by Laurie Goralka Design
Cover design by Nat Coalson

Collier Publishing
http://www.collierpublishing.com

This book is dedicated to Colorado

— its people, its landscape, its future

About the Author

Grant Collier has been working as a professional photographer and writer since 1996. His work has been featured in magazines throughout the United States and Europe, and he is the author of the large coffee-table book *Colorado: Moments in Time.* Grant is a life-long resident of Colorado and currently resides in Lakewood.

Acknowledgments

I would like to give special thanks to Ed and Nancy Bathke, who lent me some of the images from their fine collection of Joseph Collier photographs, to Catamount Mayhugh, who helped me locate some of the photographs, and to Dax Oliver, who gave me feedback on portions of the text.

I would also like to thank my parents, Bud and Nancy Collier, my sister, Amy Stogner, the staffs of the Western History Department of the Denver Public Library, the State Historical Society, the Stanley Lake Library, and the Greeley Library, as well as Stephanie Barr, Tom Hall, Elvira Wunderlich, Jenny Noack, Phil Russell, and many others who helped in some form or another along the way.

Finally I would like to thank my aunt Mary Collier Ross and my late grandparents Malcolm E. Collier, Sr., and Kathleen Collier, who helped keep interest in Joseph Collier alive.

CONTENTS

MAP OF COLORADO

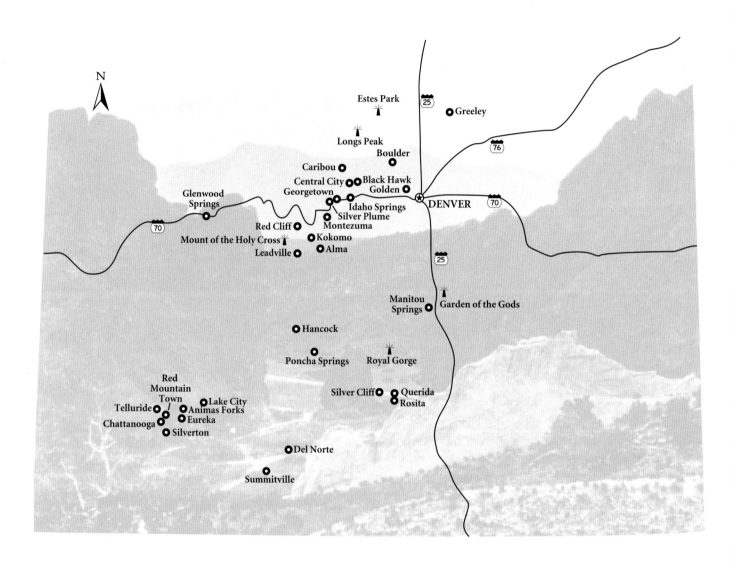

PREFACE

Writing a history book is like measuring the shoreline of a country. No matter how complete an account you give, there will always be details you have bypassed or overlooked. One must thus decide how big a measuring stick to use in documenting a region's history. In my case I have used a generously large measuring stick and have overlooked many twists, turns, and nuances in Colorado's history. For a more detailed account of any region's history, I refer you to the references at the end of this book. In particular I recommend Robert L. Brown's books on Colorado ghost towns, Muriel Sibell Wolle's *Stampede to Timberline,* and Ubbelohde, Benson, and Smith's *A Colorado History.*

What this book lacks in detailed historical accounts is hopefully made up for by the pictures that accompany each chapter. To this I must give most of the credit to my great-great-grandfather, Joseph Collier, who left Colorado a legacy of invaluable photographs. In his day he had to travel across the Rocky Mountains on foot while transporting many pounds of cumbersome photographic equipment. Today I have the much more enviable task of driving a four-wheel-drive vehicle with only a few pounds of equipment and supplies.

During the course of taking the photographs for this book, I have been asked by a number of people why I decided to undertake this project. Although the connection between me and my great-great-grandfather was certainly a factor, my primary goal was to document the changes that have taken place over the past 130 years. In the course of human lives, 130 years may seem like an extremely long period of time. But in the realm of human and geologic history, it is a tiny fraction of time. Nevertheless there have never been so many changes so quickly as there have been over the past century. Prior to the advent of modern man, change was measured in millions of years. Prior to the Industrial Revolution, change was measured in thousands of years. But today change can be measured in centuries and even decades. With such rapid progress it is necessary to occasionally look back to see where we've come from and to try to figure out where we're going.

Grant Collier
Lakewood, Colorado

INTRODUCTION

"Ugh, ouch, ugh, @#%*@, #@&*@!!!," were the first words I uttered as I scrambled up the hillside to photograph the town of Red Cliff. This was the first picture I was taking (in what has culminated in this book), and the thought of climbing another eighty some-odd hills like this one did not please me at all. Fortunately the climb at Red Cliff was one of the most difficult, but it did make me realize that my great-great-grandfather, Joseph Collier, must not have been entirely sane. When he took his picture of Red Cliff, he was carrying equipment that weighed well over fifty pounds. And the hill he climbed was no ordinary hill; parts of it were more like a cliff. I oftentimes had to take my tripod and lean it against a rock ledge above me while I edged myself up the uncomfortably steep terrain. It is possible that Joseph Collier bypassed some of the more difficult parts by climbing significantly higher up the hill and then traversing back down. Nevertheless I came to conclude that he was indeed crazy.

In taking the pictures in this book, I'd like to think that I came to know Joseph Collier as a person. Sometimes when I'd stand in the same place he did over one-hundred years ago, I'd listen closely and try to hear his thoughts. Unfortunately I never did. The only thing I really came to know were his photographs. I don't know if Joseph was a grumpy, unpleasant man or if he was a friendly, vivacious man. I also don't know what motivated him to take the pictures that he took. Perhaps it was a desire to record the early days of Colorado, so as to tell a story to future generations. Or maybe it was simply a way for him to make a living. Of course it could have been an excuse to travel around Colorado and explore the lakes and canyons, climb the mountains, and smell the wildflowers. Regardless I think that there is some sort of link between me and my great-great-grandfather. There must be a small part of him that lives on in me, and that will live on in my children, and in their children after that.

This book, of course, is not simply about me and my great-great-grandfather. It is about Colorado's past, present, and future. Before I took any photographs, I expected the towns photographed in this book to have changed dramatically. What I found is that a number of the towns have changed very little. Of course the outward appearance may be deceptive, as the communities have certainly undergone many changes that are not readily apparent.

The one thing that surprised me the most is the number of trees that exist today compared to a century ago. I knew that America's forests had recovered significantly since the turn of the century, and the photographs in this book give convincing evidence of this fact. In some of the pictures I had to slightly change the composition of the shot because there were trees in the way. In other pictures trees completely blocked the view, and I could not get a shot at all. The reason there are so many more trees today is that in the late 1800s, pioneers had the habit of clear-cutting forests and leaving the mountainsides barren. Today lumber companies use the more practical method of replanting trees after logging them.

In addition to clear-cutting forests Colorado's pioneers appear to have committed many other environmental abuses. Nearly all of the early towns in Colorado were mining towns. The pioneers mined feverishly for precious metals, with little regard for the environment. Even today Colorado's streams and rivers are being contaminated by chemicals that leak out of long-abandoned mines. The environmental abuse inflicted by the early settlers is something that few people want to consider, as it would detract from the image of rugged mountain men braving unimaginable dangers to settle a rugged and forbidding land. However it is difficult to blame the early settlers, as their standard of living was far lower than that which we enjoy today, and they had more pressing concerns than the preservation of the environment. Nevertheless we can still learn from their mistakes (as well as our own) and learn to live with the environment, rather than against it.

If there is one thing that I want readers to get from this book, it is a sense of our place in time and in space. By our place in time, I mean an understanding of the sacrifices and the blunders made by previous generations and of the obligations that we have to future generations. By our place in space, I am referring to the land on which we live and the duty we have to preserve what's left of the pristine Colorado wilderness. If we can all gain a more long-term perspective of Colorado, rather than a short-sighted vision, the future of this state will likely be even greater than its past.

◄►

CHAPTER I
JOSEPH COLLIER

JOSEPH COLLIER: Pioneer Photographer

On a cold September morning, a large, imposing figure emerges from a make-shift tent and looks around at the rugged mountain scenery. He then turns to his two companions, who are still asleep, and yells, "Let's go!"

With that they quickly rise and eat a hasty breakfast. They then load the gear onto the pack team and head for a remote mountain location.

The going is tough, as the imposing Rocky Mountains seem to resist their every move. But Joseph Collier and his men forge ahead, undaunted by the freezing temperatures and the howling wind.

After many hours they finally arrive at the summit of Burrows Park Road. Atop this high mountain pass, at an elevation of 12,650 feet, the summer seems to have given way to winter. Although his companions want to continue down to the relative comfort of Animas Forks, Collier pays little heed and begins unpacking his camera gear.

First he removes some glass plates and prepares the negatives. Then he patiently surveys the land, looking for a suitable spot to set up his tripod. A small group of travelers passes by and asks what he is doing. Collier gives them a hasty, incomplete answer and continues with his work. After some time he positions his tripod atop a rocky ledge, mounts the negative, and takes a photograph. He then carefully repositions his tripod, composes another shot, and exposes a second negative.

Although a light snow is beginning to fall and the sun is low on the horizon, Collier knows that they cannot leave just yet. Ignoring the soft grumbling of his companions, he sets up his portable darkroom, and with expert care he begins the difficult task of developing the photographs.

Finally as the darkness begins to set in, Collier and his men make their way down to the small town of Animas Forks. At the bottom the exhausted group sets up camp and lies down for a few hours of sleep. Tomorrow they will repeat the entire process all over again.

This is how I imagine Joseph Collier.

I imagine him as a strong-willed, independent man. I imagine him as a man of few words, but a man who always commanded attention. I imagine a man who at times was too demanding, at times downright unpleasant. But nevertheless I imagine a man who took pride in his craft; a man who was well respected, if not always liked; a man with a resolve and tenacity that is rarely matched.

I make these assumptions based on a few photographs and some newspaper clippings. Whether I am correct can never be determined, for very little is known about Joseph Collier, the man. Much more is known about Joseph Collier, the photographer.

As a photographer Collier took some of the finest photographs of the early scenes of

*S*elf portrait of Joseph Collier, shown in a traditional Scottish outfit, in the 1860s.
Photo courtesy Denver Public Library.

Colorado. He showed easterners, who before could only imagine, what the vast, untamed territory to the west actually looked like. And he documented the history of a land; a history that was shaped, not in decades or in centuries, but in weeks, days, and sometimes even hours. He did all of this with large, unwieldy equipment and with a new technology that few people understood.

Early in his life Joseph Collier certainly had little idea that his name would become forever linked with Colorado and the West. Born in

*J*oseph Collier prepares to take a photo of a Denver residence circa 1880.

Aberdeenshire, Scotland in 1836, Joseph Collier was trained as a blacksmith. Knowing his work ethic he likely became an expert blacksmith. However the arduous work and long hours eventually took their toll on the young Collier. In the early 1860s he suffered a debilitating back injury. While recuperating he became interested in the new field of photography. He read every book he could find on the subject, and when he had recovered sufficiently he took up the new trade.

With considerable determination Collier established himself as one of the leading photographers in the region. He opened a studio near his home in Peterhead and began photographing many of the nation's influential citizens, including the Prince of Wales, who later became King Edward VII.

Five years after taking up photography Collier moved from Peterhead to Inverness. It was here that he began experimenting with photographic enlargements. On September 4, 1868, the highly regarded British Journal of Photography wrote of these photographs:

It is no disparagement to Dr. Monckhoven, and the early pioneers in this department of photography, to say, as in all honesty we must, that in the mammoth productions of Mr. Collier, of Inverness, we find the highest excellence that we have yet seen in any enlarged photographs that have hitherto been submitted to our notice. (Mangan, *Colorado on Glass*)

Although Collier was rapidly gaining prominence throughout Europe, he, like so many of his fellow Scotsmen, dreamt of traveling to new and distant lands. He considered moving to

*J*oseph Collier sits with his tripod and camera gear circa 1890.

Australia, New Zealand, or Oregon, but on the advice of his cousin, D.C. Collier, he eventually settled on Central City, Colorado.

In June of 1871 the family — consisting of Joseph Collier, his wife Elsie Ross Collier, their four children, and "Aunt Mary" — headed to Glasgow, where they were to depart for Quebec. Before leaving, baby Mary became sick, and they were forced to leave her with her grandmother in Aberdeen. Since their tickets were non-refundable, Joseph Collier took his dog, Photo, in the baby's place.

The voyage to Quebec was a long and stormy one. When they arrived they were given the devastating news that baby Mary had died. With a heavy heart the family embarked on the Kansas and Pacific Railway for the long trip to Colorado.

Upon arriving in Denver they took the Colorado Central Railroad to Golden, and then gathered onto the Concord Coach, which carried them up Golden Gate Canyon to Central City.

It was a weary group that arrived in this rugged mining town on June 24, 1871. Not only were they still mourning the death of baby Mary, but they were met with a stark and barren landscape — a landscape that certainly did not compare to their former home of Inverness.

On the day after their arrival, D.C. Collier, who owned the *Daily Central City Register,* published the following:

Among the arrivals yesterday, were Joseph Collier and family from Inverness, Scotland. They sailed from Glasgow on May 20th, and had a very stormy passage. Mr. Collier is a cousin of one of the proprietors of the Register. (Collier, *The Photography of Joseph Collier*)

D.C. Collier not only gave the family much publicity, but he also arranged a house for them to live in. Once they got settled, Joseph Collier began establishing his photography business. In August he opened a studio behind the *Daily Register* office, and in September he set out to photograph the mining camps.

Joseph Collier poses for a photo circa 1900.

Prior to leaving, Collier packed all of his equipment, including a portable dark room, onto a team of burros. He then traveled along the Snake River and on to South Park, where he took photographs of the miners, pack teams, street scenes, and the spectacular Rocky Mountain scenery.

Collier was so impressed with the landscape that he later made several more trips to South Park and other locations throughout Colorado. During these trips Collier compiled hundreds of photographs of early scenes of Colorado. He displayed these images in his gallery and also sold them as postcards in the East.

Considering the difficulties faced by the pioneer photographers, Joseph Collier's accomplishments are quite remarkable. Before taking a photograph Collier had to prepare a negative by floating a glass plate in a solution of ether, alcohol, and other chemicals. This plate was then dipped into a solution of silver nitrate and placed into a camera, where it was exposed. The negative then had to be developed immediately, using a portable darkroom.

Once the negative was developed the photographs were printed using albumen-coated paper. This paper was held flat against the negative and then exposed to sunlight. Once an image was burned into the sheet, it was submerged into a solution of gold chloride. It was then fixed, air-dried, and attached to a cardboard backing.

Although this process would seem daunting to most photographers today, it was just one of many skills that Joseph Collier would master. Like many other early photographers, Collier also experimented with stereographs. These images were produced using a camera that contained two lenses mounted a few inches apart. The two similar, but slightly different images that were produced created a three-dimensional scene when viewed through a stereoscope.

As with his enlargements Collier quickly gained widespread recognition for his stereographs. In 1873 he presented a set of these images to the First Lady, Julia Grant, who accompanied President Ulysses Grant during their visit to Central City. Also on March 27, 1873, the *Rocky Mountain News* wrote of Collier's stereographs:

> *Some of the finest specimens of stereoscopic views we have seen are those of J. Collier, of Central City, who has made a specialty of the business for some time past. His views cover nearly every section of the Territory and are noted for their elegance of finish. The views are all taken from the most comprehensive points which gather in great variety and extent of scenery.* (Collier, *The Photography of Joseph Collier*)

Although the technology involved in producing stereographs was quite advanced, Collier always strove to push the technology even further. In 1874 he began producing stereo-transparencies. Like the stereograph, these images produced three-dimensional scenes; unlike the stereograph, the images were printed onto a glass plate, thus making the scene appear even more life-like.

On March 20, 1874, the *Daily Register* wrote of these transparencies:

Mr. Joseph Collier, the eminent photographer of Rocky Mountain scenery, has been engaged through the winter in making and perfecting appliances for doing a kind of work never before attempted in Colorado, and, so far as we know, not done elsewhere in the United States. These new pictures are called transparencies . . . We do not know the cost, but one is worth a dozen of the old kind, to one who can appreciate absolute perfection. (Mangan, *Colorado on Glass*)

With his experience in stereo-transparencies, Collier was well-positioned to take advantage of another innovation, called the sciopticion. This instrument was a modification of the less-sophisticated "magic lantern," and was a precursor to today's slide projector. It was built by placing a lamp in front of a small opening in an otherwise light-tight box. When a glass transparency was placed in front of the light, it projected the image onto a screen.

In October of 1874 Collier began preparing slides for a series of presentations, which were to be given by two professional lecturers. Following one of these lectures, the *Rocky Mountain News* wrote of Collier's images:

As exact reproductions of the scenes they purported to illustrate, they could hardly have been excelled, while as a work of art, each and every view ranked high. Not only were the buildings of local interest in our city of Denver portrayed with a fidelity to which the hearty applause of the audience continually testified, but the grand scenery of the neighboring mountains was depicted with even greater exactness. (Mangan, *Colorado on Glass*)

In addition to keeping informed of the latest technology, Collier also strove to obtain the latest photographic equipment. In January of 1872 he announced that he had received a package from London containing "the

quickest-acting photographer's lens known to science." The photographic firm of Reed and McKenney disputed this claim and declared that Collier was "humbugging the public." Collier later challenged Reed and McKenney to take part in an impartial investigation of his and their equipment. This, however, never seems to have taken place, and the controversy slowly died away.

Although competition was fierce in Central City, it began to fade in the mid-1870s. During this time many of the photographers began moving to Denver, and by 1877 only Joseph Collier remained. In the fall of that year, though, he too moved to Denver. The family bought a house at 2448 Stout, and Collier opened a gallery on Larimer Street.

At his gallery Collier took photographs of both the local citizens and the Ute Indians. He also began photographing many of Denver's homes and businesses, including churches, theatres, schools, hotels, mansions, and government buildings.

In addition to advancing his photography career, Joseph Collier also helped found the Cooperative Savings and Loan in 1885. This institution, which would later be renamed First Federal, survived until 1998, when it was bought out by Commercial Federal Bank. Although Joseph Collier was initially offered a position as vice-president, it was his son, Robert Collier, who became most closely associated with the savings and loan. In 1886, at the age of twenty-five, Robert Collier was elected attorney for the institution.

Later in 1887 he became the secretary-treasurer, a position he held until his death in 1956.

Rather than accepting a position at the firm, Joseph Collier continued working at his gallery. He took photographs of the many lavish buildings that were built throughout Denver in the late 1800s, including the Brown Palace Hotel, the Equitable Building, Union Station, and the Exposition Building. During this time Collier solidified his reputation as one of the state's leading photographers and firmly established his place in Colorado history.

Although Joseph Collier remained prolific for many years, his legacy lies primarily in the nineteenth century. Following the turn of the century Collier's health began to fail, and he was forced to abandon his livelihood. For the next ten years his condition continued to deteriorate, and on December 23, 1910, Joseph Collier passed away. He died having left behind hundreds of invaluable photographs of the early scenes of Colorado. Perhaps more important than his photographs, however, was the example that he set by the way he lived. He lived, not with fear or trepidation, but with an unyielding confidence that is rarely seen today. As a result he left a legacy that has lasted nearly 100 years, and that will continue far into the future.

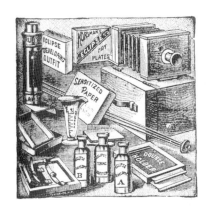

Chapter II
A Brief History
of Colorado

A BRIEF HISTORY OF COLORADO: From

Approximately 12,000 years ago, at a time when the mammoth and giant bison roamed the Great Plains, the first humans entered what is now known as Colorado. These inhabitants are known as the Paleo-Indians, and they were probably descendants of the northeastern Asian tribes who came to America via the Bering Strait some 20,000 years ago. Although not much is known about these early tribes, they are thought to have been big-game hunters, and they occupied Colorado for approximately 7,000 years.

Succeeding the Paleo-Indians in Colorado were the Archaic people, who inhabited Colorado from approximately 5000 B.C. to the time of Christ. Unlike their predecessors these inhabitants relied on small game and the gathering of wild plants to procure food.

The earliest tribe for which there is much archeological evidence is the Anasazi. These

Native Americans, who first introduced farming to the state, arrived in southwestern Colorado around the time of Christ. They constructed reservoirs to help cultivate their crops, and as their population grew they built entire villages atop the mesas in the four-corners area.

A small group of Ute Indians pose for a studio portrait. The Utes occupied western Colorado for hundreds of years prior to the arrival of the white settlers.

⧯⧯

Around 1100 A.D., for reasons not entirely known, the Anasazi moved their villages from the mesa tops to protective rock overhangs along canyon walls. They inhabited these dwellings for less than two centuries, after which they mysteriously vanished from Colorado.

*V*iew of petroglyphs on a rock wall near Del Norte, Colorado.

⧯⧯

CHAPTER II: A BRIEF HISTORY OF COLORADO

Denver to the Western Slope

Like the Anasazi, the Fremont people of northwestern Colorado also disappeared from their homeland between 1200 and 1300 A.D. This culture had occupied Colorado since approximately 400 A.D., and although some farming was introduced, they relied largely on hunting and gathering. The Fremont are perhaps best known for their impressive rock art, which can be found around much of the Western Slope.

The vacancy left by the Anasazi and Fremont Indians in western Colorado was eventually filled by the Ute Indians. The Utes occupied most of the Rocky Mountain region in Colorado, and after acquiring horses from the Spanish in the 1600s, they became one of the most powerful tribes in the western United States.

Adjacent to the Utes were the Apache, Comanche, Cheyenne, Arapaho, and Kiowa, who occupied the eastern plains of Colorado from about 1400 A.D. to 1900 A.D. Although previous Plains tribes had come to rely on agriculture, these inhabitants subsisted as hunters and gatherers.

In the mid-1600s Spanish explorers based in Santa Fe, New Mexico, began infiltrating Colorado. Although many of the tribes remained peaceful, the Comanches strongly resisted the arrival of the Spanish. They frequently raided Taos and other New Mexico settlements, and presented a constant threat to the early settlers.

Adding to Spain's troubles, French traders and explorers began penetrating the Rocky Mountain

region in the late 1600s. The two co-existed uneasily until 1762, when France ceded all of Louisiana west of the Mississippi to the Spanish.

A Ute Indian sits outside of a teepee next to a large drum.

With the French out of the picture, Spain turned its attention to the troublesome Comanche Indians. In 1779 Governor Juan Bautista de Anza led hundreds of men into eastern Colorado and soundly defeated the defiant tribe. After this devastating battle the Comanches signed a truce with the Spaniards and promised to end their raids on the New Mexico settlements.

Several men stand next to a stack of silver bricks outside the Boston & Colorado Smelting Company. The lure of silver and gold drew prospectors to remote locations throughout the Colorado territory in the nineteenth century.

Despite having gained control of much of western America, the Spanish never did colonize the northern reaches of their territory. In 1800 Napoleon Bonaparte reclaimed the Louisiana territory for France during the French Revolution. Three years later he sold this territory to the United States for approximately $15 million.

At the time the United States had little idea of what lay west of the Mississippi River. The young nation, however, had dreams of colonizing the land from coast to coast, and it quickly organized several expeditions to explore and map the newly acquired territory.

The first such expedition through Colorado was led by Zebulon Pike, who set out from Fort Belle Fontaine, near St. Louis, on July 15, 1806. In November of that year Pike and his men came within sight of the Rocky Mountains. Here they made the first American observation of an impressive 14,000 foot mountain, which would later be named Pikes Peak. After a half-hearted attempt at the summit, the party bypassed this mountain and headed deep into the Rockies. Although they failed in their primary objective of finding the source of the Red River, they did collect important information on the geography and natural resources of the region.

Following Pike in Colorado was Major Stephen H. Long, who was commissioned to find the source of the Platte, Arkansas, and Red Rivers. He and his men arrived in Colorado in June of 1820 and soon came in view of what would later be known as Longs Peak. Although they made no attempt to climb this mountain, three of Long's men did reach the summit of Pikes Peak. They then embarked on a brief journey into the Rocky Mountains, but acquired only limited information on the region.

After Long's expedition no other official expedition was sent through Colorado for many years. The area, however, was not abandoned, as fur traders and trappers began infiltrating much of the western United States in the 1820s. These now-legendary mountain men came in search of the valuable beaver pelts, which drew six to eight dollars apiece. Unfortunately, with so many trappers in search of a quick dollar, the beaver supply rapidly diminished, and by the 1840s most of the trappers were forced to abandon their livelihood. Despite their ultimate failure the knowledge that the trappers gained of the Rocky Mountains would prove invaluable in future government-funded expeditions.

The next government expedition was led by John Fremont, who was commissioned to map and survey the Oregon Trail in 1842. Following this expedition Fremont, who was guided by the famed mountain man Kit Carson, attempted but failed to locate a passable route over Colorado's Rocky Mountains.

During Fremont's third expedition to the West in 1846, the Mexican War broke out between the United States and Mexico. Mexico offered little resistance to the American troops, and by 1848 they had surrendered all of the southwestern region of the present-day United States.

Although the United States now "officially" owned this land, the Native Americans were still the primary inhabitants, and they resisted the intrusion of the white men. Inevitably, though, the power and wealth of the frontiersmen proved overwhelming, and in September of 1851 numerous tribes signed a treaty with the American settlers. The only Native Americans that remained defiant were the Utes and Jicarilla Apaches.

On Christmas Day of 1854 these tribes killed fifteen white men and kidnapped a woman and two children at Fort Pueblo. In retaliation Colonel Thomas Fauntleroy attacked and killed forty Native Americans on Poncha Pass in April, 1855. Minor skirmishes continued throughout the summer, but the Jicarilla

View of the interior of the Buell Consolidated Gold Mining and Milling Company. This structure was one of many establishments that worked ore from the mines around Central City.

Apaches and Mouache Utes finally agreed to a treaty in the fall of that year.

With most of the tribes having promised peace with the United States, the area of present-day Colorado was primed for the arrival of new settlers. Due to the remote location of the Rocky Mountains, though, nobody could have anticipated the events that would transpire in the following years.

In 1858, after hearing rumors that Cherokee Indians had discovered gold in present-day Colorado, the Russell Party, led by brothers Oliver, Green, and Levi, came west in search of a quick fortune. After several tiresome weeks they finally discovered a small patch of gold near present-day Denver. As word of their discovery

The arrival of the railroad in the 1870s brought much prosperity to Colorado. Photo courtesy Denver Public Library.

became public, the extent of their find became greatly exaggerated, and in the spring of 1859 approximately 100,000 eager prospectors set out for the Pikes Peak region of present-day Colorado. Many of these prospectors were disappointed at what they found and quickly returned home. Others remained, determined to forge a living at the base of the rugged Rocky Mountains.

The hopes of these early prospectors lay in the seemingly unlikely prospect of finding vast amounts of gold where only small amounts had previously been discovered. Fortunately in 1859 George Jackson discovered placer gold near present-day Idaho Springs, and soon afterwards John Gregory made the first discovery of lode-gold near present-day Central City.

When word of these discoveries became public, a rush of prospectors headed to the north and south forks of Clear Creek. In short time many new mining camps sprang up in the mountains above Denver. These towns set up crude forms of government, and as they matured numerous stores, schools, theaters, hotels, and churches were constructed.

As increasing numbers of settlers migrated to the mining camps, the Plains Indians became concerned that the frontiersmen were encroaching too rapidly upon their land. In 1863 and 1864 raids by these tribes on overland trails increased dramatically. The early residents became enraged by these attacks and called for action to ensure safe passage through the territory. Their demands were eventually met when, on November 29, 1864, over one hundred Native Americans were killed in what would become known as the Sand Creek Massacre. This unfortunate incident marred Colorado's reputation for many years and led to the removal of the Plains Indians from Colorado.

While Colorado was preoccupied with Native American conflicts, the Civil War was being fought in the eastern United States. In order to gain more electoral votes, the Union offered statehood to Colorado in 1864. However because of disputes between Denver and the early mining towns, this offer was ultimately turned down by the residents of Colorado.

For the early prospectors the issue of statehood was largely overshadowed by the disappearance of placer gold from many of Colorado's streambeds. These prospectors were forced to turn to hard-rock mining, which required expensive machinery and much technical expertise. Although capital began to

flow in from the East in 1863 and 1864 to finance the mines, many of the claims proved to be fraudulent, and easterners soon lost faith in the Colorado mining industry.

Adding to the miners' problems, Colorado did not yet have smelters that could adequately refine the ore from the mines. This difficulty was finally overcome in the late 1860s, when Nathaniel Hill developed a revolutionary new smelting process and built a large smelter in Black Hawk. He later moved this smelter to Denver and helped the city become the "Smelting Capital of the Rocky Mountains."

With Colorado now producing and refining ore at unprecedented levels, the only major obstacle was that of transportation. At the time Colorado was isolated from the eastern United States, and the shipment of equipment, supplies,

A large group of Ute Indians pose for a studio portrait. The Utes were driven out of Colorado following the discovery of silver and gold in the San Juan Mountains.

18

and gold was prohibitively expensive. This problem was finally alleviated in 1867-68, when the transcontinental railroad arrived in Cheyenne, Wyoming. Many had hoped that the tracks would run through Denver, but a spur line was built in 1870 to connect Denver to Cheyenne. Shortly thereafter many new lines were constructed to the neighboring mining towns, and by the 1890s railroad tracks had spread to almost every corner of the state.

With its most pressing concerns out of the way, Colorado again turned its attention to the establishment of a new state. In 1876 the Republicans needed every possible electoral vote in the presidential election and were thus quick to offer statehood to Colorado. Although disputes remained between Denver and the mining towns, the voters approved the state constitution, and on August 1, 1876, Colorado officially joined the Union. On this festive day William Byers, founder of the *Rocky Mountain News,* wrote, "Three Cheers for the State of Colorado . . . a sovereign state, mistress of herself and her destinies, Colorado will now (conquering, and to conquer,) pursue the path of prosperity."

Although Colorado looked forward to unprecedented wealth and prosperity, its mining towns still did not rival the likes of the Comstock Lode or Virginia City in Nevada. This all changed when large deposits of silver were discovered in Leadville in 1878. As news of these discoveries spread, a huge rush of prospectors converged on the area. The few who were fortunate enough to strike it rich became

A large group of pack burros stand outside the Dyer Mine. Teams such as this one were often used to transport equipment and supplies to and from the mines.

*S*everal miners and pack burros surround the North Star Mine near Silverton in the 1880s.

millionaires overnight; most others worked in difficult conditions for relatively little pay.

As more and more prospectors migrated to Leadville, the region became overcrowded, and some of the miners turned elsewhere, in search of the "next Leadville." Many new discoveries were made, and numerous mining camps were established throughout the Central Rockies. But no other silver-mining town, other than Aspen, ever did rival Leadville.

During this time some of the miners even ventured as far as the rugged San Juan Mountains. Here too they discovered large amounts of silver and gold. This area, however, was inhabited by the Ute Indians, who occupied the western third of Colorado. Due to their remote location in the Rocky Mountains, the Utes had managed to avoid conflict with the white settlers longer than most other tribes. Their fortune, however, was about to change.

In February of 1873 the Department of the Interior ordered all miners to vacate the San Juans within four months. This order was later suspended by the President, and soon afterwards a new treaty, called the Brunot Agreement, reduced the size of the Ute Indian reservation by three million acres and opened the San Juans for mining.

As it turned out the Brunot Treaty was only the beginning of the problems for the Utes. In 1879 members of the northern Utes revolted against Indian agent Nathaniel Meeker, killing him and eleven other men. This incident, which would become known as the Meeker Massacre, created an uproar throughout the state and eventually led to the removal of the Utes from Colorado.

With most of the state opened to settlement, Colorado looked with optimism towards the 1880s. Of all the cities Denver would benefit the most during this decade. It became the state capital in 1881, and its population quickly surged past 100,000. The mining towns, though still booming, lagged far behind Denver in growth. Even Leadville, due to its inhospitable climate, could not compete with Denver. Nevertheless mining remained the driving force in the state's economy. Other activities, such as industry, tourism, and farming, emerged as important factors, but all remained secondary to the prolific silver mines.

All the while gold continued to decline in importance in Colorado mining. Although it had initiated the first major rush to the Rocky Mountains, gold now lagged far behind silver in production. This finally began to change in 1890 when Bob Womack discovered gold deposits in the Pikes Peak region. Within a year a large rush of prospectors converged on what would become known as the Cripple Creek Mining District. These prospectors were not disappointed, as Cripple Creek soon became the wealthiest mining district in the state. Like Leadville it created millionaires overnight, and it produced gold at levels never before seen in Colorado.

In 1893 Cripple Creek would become even more vital to the state's economy. During this year the Sherman Silver Purchase Act, which had guaranteed the purchase of 4.5 million ounces of silver per month by the federal government, was repealed by Congress. This controversial action sent silver prices plummeting and drove Colorado silver-mining towns into a tailspin. Many of the smaller towns were simply abandoned, while the larger camps struggled to survive.

The collapse of silver prices affected not only the mining towns, but sent shock waves throughout the state. Many banks and other businesses went bankrupt in Denver, and farmers from the Western Slope to the eastern plains found nothing but falling prices for their crops. One of the few regions that remained prosperous was Cripple Creek. With the collapse of the silver-mining towns, many out-of-work miners soon flooded this district.

Like Cripple Creek, the San Juans also managed to hang on during the 1890s. Although miners here had relied largely on silver, numerous gold deposits were discovered late in the decade, and several mining towns, including Telluride,

*T*wo prospectors hope to strike it rich along a Colorado mountainside.

Ouray, Silverton, and Lake City, were able to survive these tumultuous times.

With the influx of miners to Cripple Creek, and to a lesser extent the San Juans, mine owners saw an opportunity to lower wages and increase work hours. Many of the mine workers joined the Western Federation of Miners (WFM) and were prepared to fight any action by the management. When the owners attempted to increase work hours in Cripple Creek from eight to nine, the mine workers went on strike. This strike dragged on for several months, and at one point the National Guard was called in to prevent violence. Eventually the mine owners relented, and the work-day was restored to eight hours.

CHAPTER II: A BRIEF HISTORY OF COLORADO

The victory of the mine workers in Cripple Creek gave renewed confidence to miners throughout the state. In 1896 mine workers in Leadville, also belonging to the WFM, went on strike, demanding a three dollar daily wage scale. On this occasion the mine owners gained the support of Governor Albert McIntire, and the miners were soundly defeated.

Despite their failure in Leadville the mine workers refused to relinquish hope. Another strike broke out in Telluride in 1901, and although a brief compromise was initially reached, the miners went on strike a second time in 1903. In the same year labor troubles again broke out in Cripple Creek. In both instances the mine owners emerged victorious, but only at a major cost to the state's economy.

While the hard-rock miners were involved in a bitter struggle, the coal miners east of the Rockies were fighting a battle of their own. Coal mining had emerged as a major industry in Colorado in the early 1900s, buoyed by the northern field near Boulder and the southern field near Pueblo. The men who worked in these mines endured even tougher conditions and lower pay than the hard-rock miners. They finally found some hope when the United Mine Workers moved into Colorado. After several labor disputes in the early 1900s, everything came to a head on April 20, 1914. On this fateful day the National Guard, who sided with the owners, confronted the mine workers. When the conflict was over five miners and one guardsmen had been killed, and eleven children and two women died in a fire while hiding from the violence.

After a Congressional investigation of this incident, the owners finally relented, and the coal miners gained better wages, shorter work hours, and safer working conditions. Following this strike the labor conflicts in Colorado mining towns finally came to an end. Also coming to an end, though, were the days of mining as the primary force in the state's economy. A combination of falling prices and decreasing supply brought about the ultimate demise of mining in Colorado. Although some mining towns managed to survive, none of them would ever be the same again.

View of the entrance to an early Colorado mine.

Not only was mining in Colorado changing rapidly, but the entire nation was undergoing a major transformation in the early 1900s. Gone were the days of the new frontier and the indefatigable pioneers. Also gone was the innocence of a new nation, as the U.S. found itself in the midst of the Industrial Revolution and watched anxiously as a war broke out in Europe.

When the United States finally entered this "war to end all wars" in April of 1917, Colorado residents did what they could to support the effort. Of the 43,000 Coloradans who enlisted in the army, 326 died during the war. Residents also bought war bonds, planted "war gardens," and helped organize Red Cross activities.

During the war demand for agricultural products in Europe increased dramatically. Farmers in Colorado increased their output

View of a Colorado Central Railroad train, probably in Platte Canyon.

The Arapahoe County Courthouse, which later became the Denver County Courthouse, was constructed in 1883 and demolished in 1934.

accordingly, and agriculture became the driving force in the state's economy.

When the war finally ended on November 11, 1918, residents broke out in wild celebration. This celebration was short-lived, for soon afterwards a terrible flu epidemic swept through Colorado, killing 7,783 residents. This outbreak hit the mountain towns the hardest and is reported to have killed over ten percent of the inhabitants of Silverton.

Residents would find better times in the 1920s. During this decade the automobile emerged as a part of everyday existence, and many new roads were built to allow access to all corners of the state. As agriculture began to fall off and mining continued to decline, other businesses took up the slack, and the economy became more diversified. Many residents believed

that Colorado had finally escaped the boom-and-bust cycles that had troubled earlier generations. They were badly mistaken.

Following the stock market crash of 1929, Colorado and the nation fell into The Depression. Nobody was spared by this devastating economic collapse. Banks, farms, and businesses struggled to survive, and the homeless population increased on a daily basis. Making matters worse massive dust storms hit eastern Colorado, killing crops and darkening the daytime skies.

When Franklin D. Roosevelt was elected to the presidency in 1932, he brought with him a new sense of hope for a struggling nation. Roosevelt enacted many new projects to employ the masses of unemployed workers. The biggest such project in Colorado was the Big Thompson, which was designed to transport water from the Western Slope

Several pack mules stand in a street in Ames, Colorado, near Telluride.

to the eastern valleys by way of a thirteen mile tunnel under the Continental Divide. This huge and controversial undertaking was finally completed in the 1950s at a cost of $164 million.

While some residents were employed directly by the federal government, others took advantage of the federally-sponsored gold-panning classes. Very little could be panned from Colorado's stream beds, but nevertheless these prospectors made their way back up to Central City, Black Hawk, and other old mining camps in search of any remaining gold.

The New Deal brought substantial changes to Colorado, but it did not bring an end to the Depression. This came only with the beginning of the Second World War in the 1940s. In Colorado war essentials such as coal, molybdenum, and oil were mined at unprecedented levels, and crops such as wheat and corn were grown in record quantities. In addition many new military plants and installations were constructed in the Denver-metropolitan area.

Despite the newfound prosperity the war took its toll on residents. Of the 138,800 Coloradans who joined the armed services, 2,700 would never return home. Also all nonessential mining was banned by the federal government, and gold and silver mines throughout the state, including those in Cripple Creek, were forced to close. One final dark note for Colorado and the nation was the relocation of thousands of Japanese-

Americans from the West Coast to isolated camps in the nation's interior. One of these camps, located near Granada, Colorado, held as many as 7,500 residents.

Following the end of the war in 1945, Colorado found itself in an era of new growth. In the 1940s the state's population grew from 1.1 million to 1.3 million. Much of this growth was concentrated in Denver, and it brought with it many urban problems, such as overcrowding, smog, and crime.

One factor in the state's growth was the bustling tourist industry. Many visitors were attracted to the new ski resorts, such as Vail and

The Windsor Hotel was one of many extravagant structures constructed throughout Denver in the 1880s and early 1890s.

Purgatory, that were constructed in the 1960s. Others came to the Rocky Mountains to jeep, hike, fish, or simply enjoy the impressive scenery.

Another impetus for growth came with Colorado's involvement in the Cold War. The Rocky Flats plant, located between Boulder and Golden, was built in 1953 to construct components of nuclear weapons. In addition uranium mining became a major activity on the Western Slope. Between 1948 and 1960 Colorado mined $133 million worth of uranium.

While the uranium mines flourished in western Colorado, an oil boom, spurred by the Rangely Oil Field, began east of the Rockies. This boom created much wealth for Colorado, with production reaching a high of 58 million barrels in 1956.

With all of this activity residents became concerned that the environment was being overrun too rapidly by excessive mining and tourism. Never was this pro-environmental sentiment more evident than in 1972, when residents turned down an opportunity to host the 1976 Winter Olympics. The Olympics would have brought much favorable publicity to Colorado, but residents did not want the growth and development that would accompany this event.

Although environmentalists could proclaim victory in 1972, the environmental debate in Colorado was only just beginning. In 1980 Exxon planned a $5 billion oil shale project near Grand Junction. This project would have brought incredible growth to the Western Slope and would also have brought many environmental problems, such as air and water pollution.

Unfortunately for Exxon falling oil prices and the inability to find a practical retorting method ended the company's hopes, and the project was

LODGING.

558. Union Depot Denver

CIGARS, TOBACCO ETC
BILLIARD HALL

The Union Depot was constructed in 1881 and it still stands today.

abandoned on May 2, 1982. Following Exxon's departure Grand Junction's economy fell into a tailspin. Many businesses closed down, and the population dwindled rapidly.

While the Western Slope struggled with its own economic problems, Denver began to fall on hard times in 1985. A combination of falling real estate prices, decreasing tourist revenue, and a failing oil industry led to an economic recession, which in turn led to the Savings and Loan crisis that rocked Colorado and the nation in the late 1980s. This crisis reached its climax with the failure of the huge Silverado Banking, Savings and Loan in 1988. This fiasco sunk Colorado deeper into recession and left residents fearful of the future. Fortunately, however, Colorado managed to rebound, and by the 1990s the economy had fully recovered.

With this recovery came a renewed era of growth in Colorado. This growth has been aided by the completion of the Denver International Airport in 1995 and the construction of Coors Field, the Pepsi Center, and Invesco Field at Mile High.

Although all of this development may be inevitable, it has been seen in the past that too much growth can lead to problems such as pollution, overcrowding, and desecration of some of the state's most precious landscape. Thus as Colorado moves into the twenty-first century, residents must all work together to build a future, not of suffering and disillusionment, but of promise and hope. For as Governor Roy Romer said in his inaugural address of 1987, "History will be shaped by [the people] — not by anything else."

Chapter III
The Eastern Rockies

CENTRAL CITY: The Richest Square-Mile

In January of 1859 John Gregory traveled up Clear Creek Canyon to Gregory Gulch, where he made the first discovery of lode-gold in Colorado. When word of this discovery leaked out, a huge rush of prospectors headed to present-day Central City. Many new mines were staked, and numerous buildings, including several saloons and dance halls, were constructed throughout town.

Early on the saloons and dance halls gave Central City a reputation as a very wild and unruly town. Many stories have been told of the activities in these establishments, including one that asserts that George W. Harrison shot and killed boxer Charlie Swits as he stepped out of the Barnes Pool Hall. Harrison's excuse for the murder was that he did not like Swits. Apparently the jury did not like Swits either, for Harrison was acquitted of the crime.

Harrison contributed to the early chaos in Central City, yet he also brought some culture to the town when he opened the Montana Theatre in 1862. Many shows were performed in this theatre, including one not-so-flattering play about the millionaire Pat Casey. On the opening night of this performance, Casey reportedly purchased many of the tickets, and brought several of his men to shut down the play. George Harrison responded by hiring Captain Frank Hall and fifty militia men, and the show went on as scheduled.

Although the early days were both wild and prosperous, Central City struggled during much of the 1860s. The surface ore began to disappear, and miners were forced to mine the deeper, lower grade ores. Many of the prospectors had neither the financing nor the expertise to perform this type of mining, and they were forced to sell their claims to wealthier individuals and companies.

The arrival of the new mine owners brought a calming influence to the community. Many of the new residents brought their wives and children, and several schools and churches were constructed. In addition another structure, called the Teller House, was built by the millionaire Henry M. Teller in 1872. This establishment quickly gained a reputation as one of the finest hotels in the West, and it attracted many influential visitors, including President Ulysses S. Grant. Prior to Grant's arrival in 1873, the residents of Central City reportedly laid a pathway of silver bricks leading to the Teller House for the President to walk on.

Central City's rapid growth came to a halt following a devastating fire in May of 1874. While a few structures, including the Teller House, were spared, most of the buildings were destroyed.

on Earth

They were subsequently rebuilt using stone or brick, and many of them survive today.

In addition to the fire Central City was also hampered by grasshopper plagues in 1874 and 1875, and by an outbreak of diphtheria in 1879. Nevertheless the community persevered, and the mines continued to pour forth large amounts of gold.

Central City's economy was also supported by the arrival of the Colorado Central Railroad in 1878. Although this railroad reached Black Hawk in 1872, it took several years to complete the line to Central City, as the town was 500 feet higher than Black Hawk. This difficulty was finally overcome by constructing over three miles of loops and switchbacks in order to gain altitude for the trek to Central City.

Unfortunately the railroad could not prevent Central City's rapid decline in the 1880s. Many of the richest mines became depleted, and numerous residents returned to Denver or headed to the boom town of Leadville.

Over the next several decades Central City's economy continued to deteriorate. Mining continued on a limited basis well into the twentieth century, but Central City remained only a ghost of its former self. The economy did not begin to recover until 1932 when the Opera House was reopened and an annual summer festival was established. Central City also benefited in the 1950s when Colorado residents became interested in historic preservation. Some of these people turned their attention to Central City's historic buildings, and as a result many nineteenth century structures remain standing today.

In order to raise money to continue this preservation effort in Gregory Gulch and around the state, gambling was introduced to Central City in 1991. Although several residents were reluctant to allow casinos to infiltrate Central City, many of them felt that the preservation of the region's history outweighed their concerns over gambling. Phil Russell, a resident of Central City since 1944, echoed these thoughts when he said of gambling, "It has raised taxes and ruined businesses that are not involved in gambling. But it has been very good as far as keeping the place clean and renovated."

Although gambling appears to have been beneficial for Central City, residents must not lose sight of the initial goal of preserving and restoring historic structures throughout the state. Regardless of what one may think of gambling, it is hard to argue that the preservation of Colorado's rich heritage is not a worthwhile objective.

Central City, shown in the early 1870s, was the site of the first lode gold discovery in Colorado.

CHAPTER III: THE EASTERN ROCKIES

Today Central City continues to draw large numbers of gold-seekers. The gold they seek, however, lies in the casinos not the mountains.

*I*n the 1870s Central City was known as "The Richest Square-Mile on Earth." Photo courtesy Denver Public Library.

CHAPTER III: THE EASTERN ROCKIES

*A*lthough it can no longer make such bold claims, Central City found renewed prosperity in the 1990s.

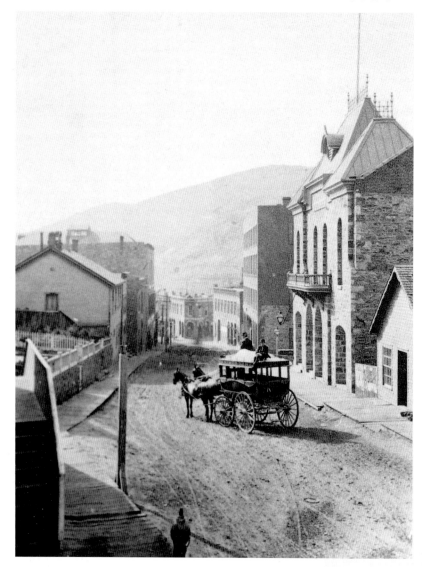

The Teller House and Opera
House, shown on the right,
were two of Central City's
finest buildings.

The same scene along
Eureka Street in 1997 shows
surprisingly few changes.

*V*iew of Central City in the 1870s. A Colorado Central Railroad engine lies in the foreground.

*T*oday the railroad line has been torn down and only a small service road remains.

In 1874 Central City was devastated by a severe fire that destroyed most of the town's buildings.
Photo courtesy Denver Public Library.

*F*ollowing the fire most of the structures were rebuilt using stone or brick and many of them survive today.

*I*n the 1870s Main Street in Central City was the center of business activity.
Photo courtesy Colorado Historical Society.

Today Main Street is inundated with casinos and tourists.

BLACK HAWK: The Mill City of the Rockies

Following John Gregory's gold discovery in 1859, a large rush of prospectors headed to Gregory Gulch. Some mines were staked near Black Hawk, and many more claims were made around Central City and Nevadaville. Black Hawk nevertheless benefited from these discoveries, as many mills and smelters were constructed around town.

Early on the mills brought much prosperity to Black Hawk, and by the mid-1860s the community had a school, a church, a newspaper, six groceries, thirteen saloons, a brewery, and a cracker factory.

Due to this rapid growth many of the trees on the surrounding hillside were logged for use in construction and as a source of fuel. As a result the runoff from spring rains came directly into Gregory Gulch, and Black Hawk was flooded several times. This problem was ultimately resolved when residents constructed a rock flume below the sidewalks at a cost of $32,000.

Another difficulty for Black Hawk resulted from its inability to handle the lower-grade ore from the mines. This finally changed in the late 1860s when Nathaniel Hill built the Boston & Colorado Smelting Works. This smelter employed some of the latest technology and helped rejuvenate the economy.

Black Hawk received another boost in 1872 when the Colorado Central Railroad arrived in town. This railroad, which ran until 1941, helped the community grow and prosper throughout the 1870s.

Despite the early prosperity Black Hawk fell on hard times in the 1880s. Much of the richer ore from the neighboring mines became depleted, and many of the residents left town.

Throughout much of the twentieth century Black Hawk continued to decline. The economy did not recover until the introduction of gambling in 1991. In the following years thousands of residents began rushing up to Gregory Gulch in search of a quick fortune. Like the gold rush in 1859, this rush has brought much wealth to Black Hawk, and it should ensure continued growth and prosperity well into the twenty-first century.

Black Hawk, shown in the 1870s, was an important milling and smelting center.

*B*lack Hawk, shown in 2000, is now a prosperous gambling town.

The Colorado Central Railroad, shown in the 1870s, was built up Clear Creek Canyon from Golden. The left fork connected with Idaho Springs, while the right fork followed North Clear Creek to Black Hawk.

CHAPTER III: THE EASTERN ROCKIES

*T*oday, the railroad tracks have been replaced by Highway 6 and Highway 119, which follow the same route.

CARIBOU: Where the Winds Were Born

While hunting in the mountains in 1860, Sam Conger noticed some unusual rock formations near present-day Caribou. He stopped for a moment to observe these outcroppings and then continued in pursuit of a large elk. Eight years later Conger noticed some similar rocks in Wyoming and was told that they contained silver deposits from the rich Comstock Lode in Nevada.

Although it was nearing winter Conger immediately returned to Colorado and began searching for the rocks he had seen eight years before. He waded through deep snow and endured freezing temperatures, oftentimes struggling just to survive.

Finally in the spring of 1869 Conger discovered a small patch of silver ore. Faced with the vast, uninhabited expanse of mountains before him, Conger realized that he would need help in his search for the mother-lode. In August of 1869 he returned with five men, and they soon discovered the Caribou Mine, which would go on to produce $8 million in silver.

Conger and his men tried to keep their discovery a secret, but word of their find quickly leaked out, and in the summer of 1870 numerous prospectors converged on the area. A new town rapidly emerged, and on September 26 Caribou was incorporated.

By 1871 Caribou had several hotels and boarding houses, five grocery stores, three bakeries, and four saloons. Many new silver discoveries were made, and Caribou became one of the richest mining towns in northern Colorado.

In spite of its prosperity Caribou was surely one of the most inhospitable places to live in all of Colorado. Located along a barren mountainside at an elevation of 9,905 feet, it became known as "the town where winds are born." On the worst days miners had to crawl on their hands and knees against the fierce winds just to get to work.

In the winter, which lasted nearly nine months, huge snowdrifts would build up around town. Occasionally the drifts became so high that visitors had to enter through second story windows of the Sherman House in order to reach their rooms.

When the snows finally receded in the summer, Caribou was subject to severe thunderstorms. Many cattle were killed when lightning repeatedly struck this defenseless town. Only after it was abandoned was it discovered that Caribou had been built atop a huge dike of iron.

Despite the natural hazards Caribou's mines continued to produce large amounts of silver, and the economy thrived throughout much of the 1870s. In 1879, though, two epidemics of scarlet fever and diphtheria ravaged the community. Numerous residents died, including many children.

Later that same year a devastating fire swept through town, destroying many of the buildings. Although some of the structures were rebuilt, this fire signaled the beginning of the end for Caribou.

The Panic of 1893 was yet another staggering blow for Caribou. Many residents left town, and the population dwindled rapidly. Later in 1895 the decisive blow was struck, as a second fire raged through town. The only buildings that were spared were the church and two hotels.

By 1900 Caribou's population had fallen to forty-four. For those who remained the devastation was not quite complete, as an earthquake shook the town in 1903 and a third fire destroyed the remaining business structures in 1905.

Through the early decades of the twentieth century, Caribou clung tenaciously to existence. In 1944 the last permanent resident, called "the hermit of Caribou," died, and the town officially became a ghost town.

Today Caribou is but a remnant of its former self. The once thriving community is now deserted, and all that remains are the skeletons of forgotten buildings and the persistent, howling winds that seem to bemoan the days gone by.

The wind-swept Caribou, shown in the 1870s, was one of the richest silver-mining towns in the state.
Photo courtesy Denver Public Library.

Caribou is now deserted and all but a few of the buildings have succumbed to the ravages of time.

IDAHO SPRINGS: Site of George Jackson's

In January of 1859 prospector George Jackson was traveling along Vasquez Creek when he saw smoke rising from a nearby canyon. Believing he had come across a Ute Indian village, Jackson crept slowly towards the source of the smoke. Rather than Indians he discovered several sheep grazing near a natural hot spring.

Breathing a sigh of relief, Jackson hiked down to the junction of Chicago Creek and Clear Creek and stopped to set up camp for the night. It was here that he discovered deposits of placer gold in the streambed. Jackson quickly scooped up about nine dollars worth of this gold and headed back to Denver.

In town Jackson enlisted the help of twenty-two other men and organized the Chicago Mining Company. This group returned to Chicago Creek in May, and panned $1,900 worth of gold in one week.

Following this discovery Jackson reportedly informed John Gregory about his find and agreed to meet him at Chicago Creek. While making his way up Clear Creek, Gregory got lost and took the north fork of the river, rather than the south fork. It was here that Gregory made the first discovery of lode gold in Colorado territory.

When word of these discoveries spread, a large rush of prospectors headed up the north and south forks of Clear Creek. In short time several cabins began to spring up, and the town of Jackson's Diggings, which would later be renamed Idaho Springs, was established. Within a few months the town had ten saloons, 150 cabins, six stores, and one of the finest hotels in Colorado, called the Beebe House.

Among the early prospectors in Idaho Springs were H.A.W. Tabor, his wife Augusta, and their baby. While Tabor searched for gold his wife opened a bakery, and together they made a good living. As winter drew near an old prospector warned Tabor to take his wife back to Denver

Gold Discovery

because of the threat of avalanches. Tabor did so, and upon returning in the spring he found that the prospector had stolen his claim!

Although Tabor and other prospectors initially mined for placer gold, Idaho Springs became a major lode-mining town in the mid-1860s. It also evolved into a major smelting center and handled ore from many of the neighboring mining camps.

As it continued to grow Idaho Springs emerged as both a mining camp and a resort town. Visitors were attracted to the hot springs for their supposed medical benefits, and by 1866 the town had two bathhouses to accommodate its guests.

While Idaho Springs prospered throughout the 1860s, its economy began to falter in the 1870s. Many prospectors left town and headed to the booming silver-mining camps.

After many years of inactivity, mining finally began to pick up following the collapse of silver prices in 1893. In this year Samuel Newhouse began construction of the Newhouse Tunnel, which was driven 20,000 feet through the mountain to Central City to tap some of the richest gold deposits in the area. This tunnel allowed mining to continue in Idaho Springs until the beginning of World War II, when the government banned all non-essential mining. Since the war, only small amounts of mining have been done in the area.

Today, although the mines are closed down, Idaho Springs' economy remains strong. The town now relies on the many visitors who pass through on their way to the state's major ski areas and resort towns. In Idaho Springs the tourists can admire the many Victorian-style homes and businesses, or they can take a trip up the "Oh My God" road and view some of the region's long-abandoned mines.

Idaho Springs, shown in the 1870s, was the site of the first major gold discovery in Colorado territory.

Although a lot has changed over the years, Idaho Springs still looks much the same in 2000 as it did over a century ago.

*V*iew of the Whale
Smelting Works, west
of Idaho Springs, in
the 1870s.

*T*oday the smelter is
gone and the pace of
everyday events has
increased dramatically.

GEORGETOWN: The Silver Queen

Upon hearing the news of John Gregory's gold discovery, George and David Griffith rushed up to Central City, hoping to lay claim to some rich gold-mining property. Most of the promising claims had already been taken, so George and David left Gregory Gulch and eventually discovered the rich Griffith Lode west of Idaho Springs.

The town that sprang up around this discovery was initially called George's Town, in honor of George Griffith. Later it was combined with Elizabeth Town to the south and became known as Georgetown.

Due to the abundance of mineral deposits in the surrounding mountains, Georgetown grew rapidly, and in 1867 it became the county seat of Clear Creek County. By 1870 it had become known as "The Silver Queen," and it remained the state's leader in silver production until even larger deposits were discovered in Leadville in 1878.

In testament to its prosperity Georgetown was home to many affluent hotels and Victorian-style houses. Among the more famous buildings were the Hamill House, the Maxwell House, McClellan Hall, the Opera House, and the Barton House. The most lavish building of them all was the famous Hotel de Paris, which was built by the Frenchman Louis Dupuy.

Dupuy was one of Colorado's more colorful characters. He is said to have deserted both the French Army and the American Army, before becoming a miner in Georgetown. One day Dupuy was injured in a mining accident while reportedly saving the life of a fellow miner. Following this incident Dupuy was unable to work in the mines, and in order to make a living he started a bakery. Over the years this bakery was gradually expanded and eventually developed into the extravagant Hotel de Paris. This hotel offered some of the best furnishings, food, and wine in the nation, and it quickly became the social center of Georgetown.

In contrast to the many upscale buildings, Georgetown was also home to one of the state's more notorious red light districts, called Brownell Street. This street, which had five parlor houses and many saloons and gambling halls, was reportedly the site of numerous crimes and murders.

Despite some early violence Georgetown continued to grow and prosper in the 1870s. Its population peaked at 5,000 in 1877, the same year that the Colorado Central Railroad arrived from Denver. It was hoped that this railroad would eventually reach Leadville, but problems arose in constructing the tracks from Georgetown to Silver Plume. The distance between Silver Plume and Georgetown was only two miles, but Silver Plume was 638 feet higher than Georgetown.

In order to solve this problem Robert Blickensderfer designed a stretch of track, called the Georgetown Loop, that crossed back over itself in order to gain altitude for the trek to Silver Plume. Although the design appeared foolproof, problems arose when the Devil's Gate High Bridge was installed backwards! This error was finally corrected in 1884, and shortly thereafter the first trains began rolling into Silver Plume.

As it turned out the Colorado Central never progressed much further than Silver Plume. The Georgetown Loop, however, was not a complete failure, for it would go on to become one of the state's top tourist attractions.

Unfortunately even the Georgetown Loop could not resurrect Georgetown's economy after the repeal of the Sherman Act in 1893. Following this unpopular action by Congress, several silver mines closed down and many residents left town. By 1930 the population had fallen to 360, and in 1939 the Georgetown Loop was dismantled and used for scrap metal.

Georgetown finally began to recover in the 1950s. During this time many Colorado residents became interested in historic preservation, and some of them turned their attention to Georgetown's lavish Victorian buildings.

Among the restoration projects was the preservation of the Hotel de Paris in 1954 and the formation of the Georgetown Historical Society in 1970. The most ambitious project was completed in 1984, when the Devils Gate High Bridge was reconstructed at a cost of nearly $1 million. Today tourists can revisit a part of Georgetown's past by riding a train around the fully reconstructed Georgetown Loop.

In the 1870s Georgetown was a large and bustling silver-mining community.

Today Georgetown's economy remains strong thanks to a thriving tourist industry.

*V*iew of Georgetown from the southeast in the 1870s shows many of the town's early structures.

The same scene in Georgetown in 1999 shows moderate growth throughout the valley.

*A*lthough the Colorado Central Railroad never progressed farther than Silver Plume, the Georgetown Loop, shown in the 1880s, became one of the state's top tourist attractions.

*W*hen the Devil's Gate High Bridge was rebuilt in 1984, the Georgetown Loop reemerged as one of the state's leading tourist attractions.

*V*iew of Green Lake, above Georgetown, in the 1870s. Photo courtesy Denver Public Library.

The same view of Green Lake in 1997 shows modest changes. Guanella Pass Road lies in the foreground.

CHAPTER III: THE EASTERN ROCKIES

In the 1870s Alpine Street in Georgetown was the center of business activity. Photo courtesy Denver Public Library.

Today Alpine Street (now called 6th Street) is a popular tourist destination.

SILVER PLUME: The Miners' Town

If you come to Silver Plume and listen closely, you may be able to hear the faint melody of Clifford Griffin's violin as it echoes down from the mountains above town.

Clifford Griffin was one of our state's early pioneers. He had been engaged to be married in England, but his fiancé was found dead on the night before their wedding. In order to escape from his sorrows, Griffin moved to Colorado. He discovered the Seven-Thirty Mine and soon became one of the richest mine-owners in the region. Wealth, however, did nothing to ease his tremendous grief. Griffin lived alone in the mountains above Silver Plume, and at night he would take out his violin and play sad melodies. The miners in Silver Plume could hear the faint sounds of Griffin's violin and would often sit and listen to the music, applauding at the conclusion of each song.

One night in 1887 Griffin played an especially sad melody. At the end of the song, a gunshot rang out over the valley. The miners in Silver Plume rushed up to Griffin's cabin and found him dead in a grave he had dug out of solid rock. The men left Griffin in his grave and constructed a granite marker to honor the man that none of them really knew.

The story of Clifford Griffin is just one of many stories that could be told of this small mining town west of Georgetown. Like many other mining towns, Silver Plume had its beginnings when mineral deposits were discovered in the mountains above town.

The initial find was made by Owen Feenan, who discovered silver and lead in 1868. The town of Brownville was the first to be developed, but as mining increased, houses began to spring up in present-day Silver Plume.

As its population grew Silver Plume became one of our nation's true melting pots. Cornish, Irish, English, Italian, German, and Scandinavian families all took up residence in the area. Many of them had prior mining experience and were able to take advantage of Silver Plume's rich mineral deposits.

Among the more productive mines in the region were the Pelican, Dives, Baxter, Dunkirk, Dundenburg, Terrible, and Consolidated-Payrock Mines. The Pelican and Dives Mines were located very close to one another, and the companies were actually working from the same silver vein. As the mines moved closer together, each side accused the other of stealing from their property. The tensions slowly escalated and finally reached a climax when Jack Bishop, a mercenary of the Dives company, murdered a Pelican official. This dispute was ultimately resolved when W.A. Hamill, of Georgetown, purchased both of the mines and merged them into the Pelican-Dives Mine.

Mining disputes were just one of many problems that would plague Silver Plume. By the end of the 1880s, logging in Silver Plume and Brownville had left the mountainsides barren, and mudslides and avalanches became a problem. The mudslides were so frequent in Brownville that it was eventually abandoned, as residents began moving to Silver Plume.

Another blow for Silver Plume came with the repeal of the Sherman Act in 1893. As silver prices plummeted, several of the mines closed down and the population dwindled rapidly. Unlike many other mining towns, though, Silver Plume never did become a ghost town. Even through the toughest times, a few hardy residents always managed to hang on.

Today Silver Plume is a quiet, residential community. Many of the town's early buildings are still standing, including the Silver Plume Bandstand, Clair's Hall, the Blanton Building, Castle Hall, and the Silver Plume Catholic Church. If you should pass through, take time to view these old structures, and get a glimpse of this small town's heritage.

⋐⋑

Silver Plume, shown in the 1870s, was known as "The Miners' Town."

CHAPTER III: THE EASTERN ROCKIES

*W*ith the exception of Interstate 70, Silver Plume looks much the same in 1997 as it did a century ago.

*V*iew of Silver Plume from the east shows some of the town's early structures. Photo courtesy Denver Public Library.

CHAPTER III: THE EASTERN ROCKIES

*N*ow obscured by trees, many of the town's historic buildings remain standing today.

Chapter IV
Leadville & Vicinity

LEADVILLE: The Cloud City

At an elevation of 10,200 feet Leadville is the highest town in North America. It is a cold and barren place that is seemingly unfit for human habitation. Nevertheless it has the richest history of any mining town in Colorado.

The first gold discovery near Leadville was made by Abe Lee in 1860. Upon this discovery Lee reportedly yelled out, "Boys, I've got all California here in this pan!" Ever since then the area has been known as California Gulch.

Following Lee's discovery a large rush of prospectors converged on the area, and the town of Oro City was quickly established. Although much gold was discovered around Oro City, the prospectors were hampered by heavy black sands that oftentimes clogged their sluice boxes and made it difficult, if not impossible, to separate the gold from the gravel. As a result Oro City was abandoned after only a few years.

Despite the early difficulties prospectors W.H. Stevens and A.J. Wood came to California Gulch in 1874 and staked several claims. These men suspected that the heavy black sands that were such a burden to the early miners might contain large deposits of silver and lead. Their hunch ultimately proved correct, when in 1875 they discovered a rich vein of silver ore.

Interest in California Gulch increased rather slowly. Although a few prospectors began infiltrating the region, the real rush did not begin until 1878, when George Fryer located a rich vein of silver on what became known as Fryer Hill. In short time hundreds of prospectors began converging on Leadville, and by the end of 1879 the population had reached 18,000. Most of these individuals had no place to stay, and hundreds of them were forced to sleep in alleys, in tents, or on the floors of saloons and other business establishments.

In order to accommodate the homeless prospectors, many new buildings were quickly constructed throughout town. By May of 1879 Leadville had nineteen hotels, forty-one lodging houses, eighty-two saloons, thirty-eight restaurants, seven smelting and reduction works, twenty-one gambling halls, and an unspecified number of dance halls.

Many of the trees on the surrounding mountains were logged for use in construction and as a source of fuel. As a result the price of lumber began to soar. The prices of other goods, such as hay and coal, also became extremely inflated, due to the high cost of transportation to and from Leadville.

Despite the exorbitant prices prospectors continued to pour into Leadville by the thousands. Many were drawn by stories of those who hit it rich overnight. The most famous such story was that of Horace Tabor, who made his initial fortune on the Little Pittsburgh. Tabor later purchased the Matchless Mine, which went on to become one of the region's biggest producers. For a while it appeared as though Tabor could do no wrong. A story is told that Chuck Bill Lovell, who owned a claim called the Chrysolite, salted the property using ore from Tabor's Little Pittsburgh Mine. He then sold the claim to Tabor and walked away with a handsome profit. Tabor, however, would have the last laugh, for he refused to give up on the claim and eventually struck silver.

Others who hit it big include John Morrissey, August Riche, George Hook, Pat Gallagher, Jack McCombe, Pete Breene, Alva Adams, Samuel Newhouse, George Robinson, "Judge" Pedery, and the "Unsinkable" Molly Brown, whose husband made a fortune here. Even some who were not directly involved in mining became millionaires. Charles Boettcher, who would later invest in the Brown Palace Hotel, made his initial fortune from a hardware store in Leadville. Meanwhile David May opened a dry goods store, which later became the Mays Department Store Company. Also the Guggenheims made much of their fortune on a smelter, called the American Smelting and Refining Company.

Although some struck it rich overnight, many others fared far worse. Hundreds of men are said to have died due to the freezing temperatures and the lack of adequate food and shelter. Others died from the violence and chaos that oftentimes erupted in the boisterous mining town. Much of this violence occurred along State Street, which quickly emerged as one of the state's most notorious red-light districts. Residents were reluctant to walk down this street alone at night, and legend says that those who did usually carried a loaded pistol in each hand.

Many stories have been told of the activities along State Street. One such story asserts that a first-time gambler, who had ventured into a gambling hall along State Street, lost all of his money and nearly all of his possessions in a game of poker. He became so distraught that he reached into his pocket for his gun, intending to take his life, but he found instead a meerschaum pipe. He promptly sold the pipe, reentered the game, and eventually won $4,800. Now thankful just to be alive, he asked for a Bible and swore on it never to gamble again.

Despite the early chaos Leadville did, with time, begin to settle down. At first preachers were forced to give their sermons on the streets, but in time many churches and a school were constructed. In addition several lavish buildings, including the Tabor Opera House and the Tabor Grand Hotel, were built throughout town. But Leadville never did shake its image as one of the wildest communities in the West.

Although the early days saw unprecedented wealth and prosperity, this all came to an end following the Panic of 1893. As silver prices plummeted millionaires lost their fortunes overnight, and miners vacated Leadville in droves. The town's streets, which were once bustling with activity, became quiet, and many of the houses were torn down and used for firewood.

One of the hardest hit during this time was Horace Tabor, who had invested his fortune throughout Colorado. Following the collapse of silver prices, Tabor lost nearly everything he owned. When he died in 1899 he told his second wife, Baby Doe, to hold onto the Matchless Mine, as he was convinced that it still held vast fortunes. Baby Doe did so faithfully, and actually took up residence at a claim near the mine shaft. In 1935 her body, dressed in rags, was found frozen inside a tool shed at the mine.

While the millionaires struggled to get by, other residents fared even worse, and Leadville continued to decline. In order to help rejuvenate the economy and attract tourists, the town leaders constructed the Leadville Ice Palace during the winter of 1895-96. This enormous structure, which cost $40,000 to build, covered five acres and was fifty feet high. It was made of eight-foot blocks of ice, and it contained several ballrooms, a restaurant and lounge, and a skating rink.

Despite its tremendous size the ice palace proved to be a huge failure. In March the warm Chinook winds blew in to Leadville, and the immense structure began to melt. By June it was forced to close, and soon afterwards it completely melted away.

To make matters worse the miners in Leadville went on strike in 1896, demanding a three dollar wage scale. In order to prevent the owners from opening the mines with imported workers, the union miners began sealing off some of the roads and sabotaging the mines. In response Governor McIntire sent in troops to maintain order. The troops allowed the mine owners to reopen the mines with non-union workers, and the strike soon came to end.

Although the miners returned to work, Leadville's silver mines would never fully recover. During the early twentieth century, many of the mines closed down, and the population continued to decline.

Mining finally began to pick up again when the Climax Molybdenum Mine began producing molybdenum for use during World War I. This mine, which was located approximately twelve miles northeast of Leadville, remained open until the mid-1980s, when it gradually ceased operation. Today the huge tailings ponds produced by the mine are being cleaned up by the Climax Molybdenum Company, as part of an extensive reclamation project.

While the molybdenum mine closed down, another mine, called the Black Cloud, continued to operate throughout the 1990s. This mine was finally shut down on January 29, 1999, thus ending the long and storied history of mining in Leadville.

Although the mines are now closed down, they are still an integral part of the community. Many of them are being cleaned up by the Environmental Protection Agency, as acid runoff from the abandoned mineshafts has been contaminating the area's water supply. This clean-up effort has sparked a debate between those in favor of historic preservation and those in favor of environmental restoration. Although the two may appear mutually exclusive, it seems possible that a reasonable compromise can be reached, ensuring that the history of the region can be preserved, without posing significant threats to the environment.

◄▣►

*I*n the 1880s State Street in Leadville was one of Colorado's most notorious red-light districts.

*I*n contrast to its more boisterous days, State Street (now called 2nd Street) is a quiet and peaceful neighborhood.

*T*oday mining has come to an end in Leadville and the economy is supported by tourism.

*L*eadville, shown in the 1880s, was a large and unruly mining community.

No. 276. CHESTNUT STREET — LEADVILLE.

CHAPTER IV: LEADVILLE & VICINITY

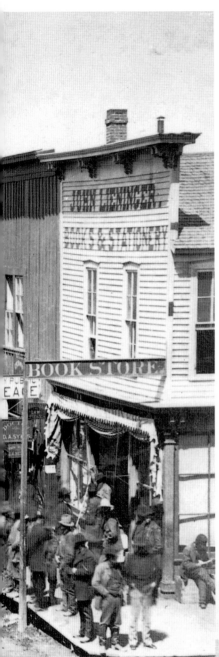

*C*hestnut Street, shown in the 1880s, was the center of business activity.

*O*ver the years Chestnut Street (now called 3rd Street) has changed considerably.

MONTEZUMA: Site of the First Silver

In 1863 prospector John Coley traveled from South Park to Glacier Mountain, where he made the first silver discovery in the territory of Colorado. This find set off a small rush of prospectors to the high and rugged mountains in Summit County, Colorado.

Amongst these prospectors were M.O. Wolf, Henry M. Teller, and D.C. Collier. These men conceived of establishing a small town in the beautiful valley where they were camped. D.C. Collier, who was instrumental in founding the town, gave it the name Montezuma, after the late Aztec Emperor of Mexico.

Due to its remote location in the Rocky Mountains, the early days in Montezuma were tough, and the population grew slowly. Only with the construction of Webster Pass and Argentine Pass did the town start to take off.

By 1880 Montezuma had a post office, three hotels, a schoolhouse, a sawmill, a smelter, and a population of approximately 800 people. Although this was probably the peak year for Montezuma, the economy remained strong throughout the 1880s and into the 1890s.

Over the years several interesting stories have been told of Montezuma. One concerns a professional gambler who had made his way across the state, amassing hundreds of dollars in winnings. The gambler's last stop was in Montezuma, where he convinced some of the residents to join him in a game of poker. Within a few hours everyone had dropped out except the gambler and a man named T.R. Newman. These two men played into the wee hours of the night, and in the morning the gambler was seen walking out of town, for he no longer had fare for the stage.

Discovery

Another story concerns two prospectors who were in love with the same woman in Missouri. The two men were saving their money so that they could return to Missouri and impress their lady-love. Eventually one of the men grew impatient, and he killed his adversary and stole his money. The man then returned to Missouri, but upon arriving he was captured and brought back to Montezuma. The justice of the peace prepared to hang him, but before he could do so the murderer escaped and was never seen again.

Whereas the early days in Montezuma were certainly eventful, they were not without their difficulties. Following the repeal of the Sherman Act in 1893, Montezuma's economy fell into a tailspin. Although the town managed to survive, it would never fully recover.

In the twentieth century Montezuma continued to decline. By 1956 the population had fallen to twelve, and the future did not appear promising. However in 1957 the construction of the Roberts Tunnel, as part of the Denver water system, helped rejuvenate the economy. Workers on the project took up residence in Montezuma, and the population rose to seventy-five.

Unfortunately this resurgence was short-lived for in December of 1958 a flash fire swept through town. This fire destroyed a hotel, the town hall, six garages, and left nearly half of the population homeless.

After all that residents had endured, they were not willing to give up. The town managed to rise from the ashes and is still standing today. Montezuma is now a popular destination for many tourists who come to jeep, hike, bike, and ski in the spectacular mountains above town.

*I*n the 1870s Montezuma was a small silver-mining community. Photo courtesy Colorado Historical Society.

*A*lthough it has endured many difficult times, Montezuma has survived to the present day.

View of Montezuma in the 1870s with Collier Mountain on the left, Teller Mountain on the right, and the Snake River in the foreground.

The same scene in Montezuma today shows the Snake River, but the town itself is obscured by trees.

View of Montezuma
in the 1870s with
Glacier Mountain in
the background.
Photo courtesy
Denver Public Library.

The same scene in
Montezuma in 1997 shows
only minor changes.

ALMA: Site of the Espinosa Murders

While Hollywood's version of the Old West as a place of thieves, murderers, and con men is largely fictional, there certainly were instances in which this portrayal is accurate. A good example is the crusade of the notorious Espinosa brothers. These Mexican brothers, who had a deep hatred for all Anglo-Americans, killed six of their estimated thirty-two victims in the area between Alma and Red Hill.

Although a large bounty was placed on their heads, the Espinosa brothers managed to avoid capture for several years. Eventually the famed mountain man Tom Tobin and a group of miners surrounded and killed the Espinosa brothers, thus ending one of the darker episodes in Colorado's history.

Not long after the Espinosa murders, placer gold was discovered in Alma, initiating a small rush to the area. The town was incorporated in 1872, and by 1873 it had a population of 500.

The early days saw a small measure of prosperity and the town really took off in 1879, when large deposits of silver were discovered on nearby Mt. Bross and Mt. Lincoln. These discoveries brought about a second rush to the area, and allowed Alma to grow and prosper throughout the 1880s.

In testament to its wealth Alma had a newspaper, several hotels, and a population of approximately 1,000 people. It also had a smelter, which worked ore from many of the neighboring mines.

Unfortunately Alma's peak years were short-lived for the town was hit hard by the Panic of 1893. Somehow it managed to survive and mining continued throughout the decade and into the twentieth century.

In 1937 Alma was devastated by a fire that swept through the main business district. The blaze started in a beer parlor and then spread to adjacent buildings. When it was over the fire had destroyed a pool hall, a barber shop, a restaurant, several stores, and the Getley Motor Company, which housed most of the town's automobiles.

In testament to the residents' perseverance, much of the town was rebuilt, and Alma still stands today. Although Mt. Bross and Mt. Lincoln are no longer mined, they are still of great value to the community. Today people come from all over the state to explore these impressive 14,000 foot peaks. From the top one can gaze across South Park and down at the small town of Alma, both of which look nearly the same as they did over one hundred years ago.

ALMA

The town of Alma, shown in the 1880s, grew rapidly after silver deposits were discovered on nearby Mt. Bross and Mt. Lincoln. Photo courtesy Denver Public Library.

*A*lma has survived throughout the 20th century, and its economy is now supported by tourism and mining.

KOKOMO: Once a Mining Town, Now a Tailings Pond

While on their way to the boom town of Leadville, a group of prospectors is said to have gotten caught in a terrible snowstorm at the base of the imposing Ten Mile Range. The freezing cold and heavy snows took their toll on the group, and one member of the party did not survive. While stopping to bury their companion, the group is said to have discovered rich silver deposits in what would become known as the Dead Man Mine.

Although this story does have much literary appeal, it is generally believed that the first discoveries were made by the Recen brothers during the winter of 1878-79. These brothers are known to have played a pivotal role in founding both Kokomo and the neighboring town of Recen.

Following the initial discovery many prospectors rushed to Kokomo and numerous mines were staked, including the rich Crown Point and Ruby Silver Mines. The town grew rapidly, and by the early 1880s it had a church, a bank, three newspapers, numerous stores, and a school.

Kokomo's growth was interrupted in 1882, when a terrible fire swept across Ten Mile Avenue. Following this disaster the residents of Recen offered free lots to those who had lost their homes or businesses, and the two towns officially merged. The post office retained the name Kokomo, but the town was called Recen.

In the 1890s Recen was served by both the Denver & Rio Grande and the Denver, South Park and Pacific Railroads. By this time, though, the town had begun to decline. It managed to hang on for several more decades but would never fully recover.

In 1965 the Climax Molybdenum Company bought the former townsites of Kokomo and Recen, and used the land to dump tailings from a nearby molybdenum mine. These tailings ponds have grown to tremendous proportions and now cover several old mining towns. Although the company does have extensive reclamation plans, the former townsite of Kokomo will never be the same.

Kokomo, shown in the 1880s, was a typical mining town.

Today Kokomo is buried beneath the Climax Molybdenum Company's huge tailings ponds. Due to restricted access, exact duplication of the historic photo was impossible.

PONCHA SPRINGS: The Resort Town

oncha Springs was founded in 1879 by James True, who saw the advantages of laying out a supply camp amongst many up-and-coming mining towns. True opened a bank in Poncha Springs, and in a short time many other businesses, including several resorts, sprang up around town.

The resorts were built to attract visitors to the nearby hot springs. Many people believed that the hot springs had miraculous healing powers, and numerous sick and disabled people came in hopes of a cure.

Early on Poncha Springs appeared to be a quiet and peaceful town, devoid of the criminal activity associated with the mining camps. However in 1881 James True's bank was set on fire. True, who had grown distrustful of many of his business associates, accused one of his adversaries of arson and shot and killed him.

Following this incident True was charged with murder, and the case went to court. The murdered man's friends accused True of setting fire to his own bank in order to cover up the bank's losses. The jury, however, sided with True, and he was acquitted.

Not long after this incident a larger fire consumed most of the town's homes and businesses. Although tourists continued to visit the hot springs, the town itself was slow to recover.

Today Poncha Springs has reemerged as a supply center. Rather than supplying the miners and prospectors, it supplies the tourists and vacationers who pass through while on their way to the state's ski areas and resort towns.

Poncha Springs, shown in the 1880s, was established as a supply town to the neighboring mining camps. The official town site lies in the background. Photo courtesy Denver Public Library.

The same scene in 1998 shows a summer camp in the foreground. The town of Poncha Springs, located in the background, continues to function as a supply camp.

View of Poncha Springs in the 1880s shows Mt. Shavano
and Mt. Antero in the background.

The same view in 1998
shows only modest
development in the valley
below the mountains.

HANCOCK: From Railroad Town to Ghost Town

The town of Hancock was established in 1880 as a home for workers on the Alpine Tunnel. This tunnel, which was built to bypass rugged mountain passes, was constructed by the Denver & South Park Railroad at a cost of $100,000 per mile.

In addition to the railroad Hancock also experienced a small mining boom. The biggest producer was the Stonewall Mine, which was discovered in 1879. Other mines in the region included the Allie Belle, the Flora Belle, and the Hancock Placer Claim.

By 1881 Hancock had five stores, a hotel, several saloons, two sawmills, and a population of several hundred people. In November of that year the Alpine Tunnel was completed and many trains began rolling through town.

As it turned out the tunnel was a financial disaster for the Denver & South Park Railroad. Even after it was completed the company had to employ workers to clear the snow and rock slides that oftentimes blocked the tracks above Hancock.

Due in part to these difficulties, Hancock's peak years were short-lived. Although the town survived into the twentieth century, only a few hardy prospectors remained. Finally in 1926 the last passenger train left town, carrying with it Hancock's only remaining residents.

In the 1880s Hancock was home to workers on the Alpine Tunnel.

*T*oday evidence of the former town site has almost completely vanished.

RED CLIFF: The First Seat of Eagle County

In 1878 two prospectors from Leadville discovered silver deposits in what became known as the Little Ollie Mine. When word of this discovery leaked out, a rush of prospectors headed to the area, and the town of Red Cliff was quickly established.

Within a few years Red Cliff had five hotels, a post office, a school, numerous saloons, an opera house, and a newspaper. It quickly emerged as the largest town in the region, and it became the county seat of Eagle County in the mid-1880s.

Not long after Red Cliff was incorporated, the Ute Indians revolted against Nathan Meeker, killing him and eleven other men at the White River Ute Indian Agency. Following this massacre the residents of Red Cliff became fearful of an Indian attack, and they constructed a log fort to protect the women and children. Although this fort was never used, it probably served its purpose in giving the residents some peace of mind.

While Red Cliff was protected against potential Indian attacks, it could not protect itself against Mother Nature. Early on several fires ravaged the community, including three in one month in 1883. In addition many devastating avalanches came roaring down the red-quartzite cliffs that gave the town its name. Nevertheless Red Cliff always managed to rebuild, and the town continued to grow and prosper during the 1880s.

Red Cliff's growth was aided by the arrival of the Denver & Rio Grande Railroad in 1881. Although a spur line was planned up Homestake Creek from Red Cliff, this project was eventually abandoned. The railroad survey crews, however, discovered gold deposits along the creek, and Red Cliff benefited by becoming the supply center to the many up and coming mining camps.

While many of the neighboring mining towns have long since been abandoned, Red Cliff has survived to become one of the few permanent settlements in the district. Today it is a quiet town, nestled amidst some of the finest scenery in the state.

*A*t its peak in the 1880s Red Cliff was the county seat of Eagle County.

*W*hereas many of the neighboring towns have been abandoned, Red Cliff has survived throughout the twentieth century.

GLENWOOD SPRINGS: Site of "The Spa"

Prior to the arrival of the frontiersmen, the hot springs at present-day Glenwood Springs were inhabited by the Ute Indians. The Utes viewed the springs as a sacred place with miraculous healing powers, and called them "Yampah," meaning "Big Medicine."

The first American to view the hot springs was Captain Richard Sopris, who had become ill during his travels across Colorado in 1860. Sopris remained at the springs for several days while recuperating in the hot waters. While there he named the area Grand Springs.

Although an occasional trapper passed through Grand Springs in the following years, the Utes remained the primary inhabitants until 1879. In this year James M. Landis built a small cabin near the springs. About the same time Isaac Cooper came to Grand Springs in search of a cure for the many ailments he had acquired during the Civil War. He too was impressed with the region, and in 1882 he bought Landis' claim for $1,500.

Cooper, who helped found the town of Glenwood Springs, envisioned converting the area into a grand resort center, where people from all over the world would come to experience the miraculous curative powers of the springs. However his plan was slow to take off, and Glenwood Springs remained a remote, seldom-visited region of Colorado.

Cooper finally received a break during the severe winter of 1883. Due to the heavy snows and

freezing temperatures, miners from the neighboring town of Carbonate were forced to wait out the winter in Glenwood Springs.

In the following spring the high water from melting snow stranded most of the miners until summer. By the time they were able to leave, many of the inhabitants had grown accustomed to life in Glenwood Springs and chose to take up permanent residence.

At first Glenwood Springs was simply a "tent city," but in short time a school, a blacksmith shop, a restaurant, two grocery stores, a dance hall, and several saloons and gambling halls were constructed. In addition many farms were established throughout the valley, and agriculture emerged as the town's primary industry.

One of the important figures in the early history of Glenwood Springs was Walter Devereux. Devereux had made a fortune in silver and coal mining, and he came to Glenwood Springs to invest some of that fortune. Like Isaac Cooper, Devereux had dreams of building a grand resort center around the hot springs. Unlike Cooper, Devereux had the capital to finance his dreams.

In 1886 Devereux founded the Glenwood Electric Company, and Glenwood Springs became one of the first hydro-electrically lighted towns in the nation. Later in 1888 he formed the Glenwood Water Company, which supplied running water to the town.

Another important step in the development of Glenwood Springs was the arrival of the Denver

& Rio Grande Railroad on October 5, 1887. The railroad, which was built through Glenwood Canyon at a cost of over $2 million, arrived in Glenwood Springs amidst wild cheers from the town's residents.

Just two months later, on December 12, the Colorado Midland Railroad also arrived in Glenwood Springs. This event was tempered by the death of Isaac Cooper just ten days earlier. Cooper's body was laid in state in the lavish Hotel Glenwood, and all businesses were closed so that residents could pay their final respects to the town's founder.

Shortly before his death Cooper had sold the Yampah Hot Springs to Walter Devereux for $125,000. With this property Devereux planned to build a huge resort center, called "The Spa." The first task was to redirect the Colorado River around the hot springs in order to make room for a 615- by 75-foot pool. The pool, called the Natatorium, was completed in 1888. Two years later an extravagant stone bathhouse was built to complement the spa.

Devereux's final project was completed in 1893, when the famous Hotel Colorado opened for business. The hotel was one of the finest in the nation, and it attracted tourists from all over the world.

In addition to tourism Glenwood Springs also relied on ranching and farming in the early twentieth century. These industries allowed Glenwood Springs to survive, even as tourism began to decline at the beginning of World War I.

During the war several of Glenwood Springs' residents enlisted in the 89th Division, which saw active duty in Europe. Later, during World War II, Glenwood Springs was infiltrated by the troops stationed at nearby Camp Hale. Amongst these troops was the famous 10th Mountain Division. Although these men sustained heavy casualties during the war, they performed admirably and were instrumental in the allied victory.

Following World War II Glenwood Springs entered a period of steady growth. One factor in this growth was the approval of Interstate 70 through Glenwood Springs in 1967. The last four-lane stretch of highway along this interstate was finally completed through Glenwood Canyon in 1992.

Another event of note in recent times was the tragic death of fourteen firefighters in the Storm King Mountain fire in 1994. These brave individuals lost their lives while trying to save the homes and businesses of Glenwood Springs, and residents will surely long remember their sacrifices.

Despite the recent tragedy residents of Glenwood Springs look forward to a bright future. With traffic continually increasing along I-70, Glenwood Springs is well positioned to reap the rewards of a growing Colorado tourist industry well into the twenty-first century.

Glenwood Springs, shown in the 1880s, was a prominent resort center. Photo courtesy Denver Public Library.

*G*lenwood Springs, shown in 1999, remains a popular tourist destination.

Chapter V
The San Juans

SILVERTON: The Town that Never Quit

Long before white men set foot on the San Juan Mountains, the Ute Indians inhabited this rugged and forbidding land. Arriving in Colorado between 500 and 800 years ago, the Utes lived isolated and relatively peaceful lives. Unlike other tribes who had come to rely on agriculture, the Utes used the more traditional hunting and gathering methods to procure food. They were among the first Native Americans to acquire horses from the Spanish and became both feared and respected by neighboring tribes.

When the miners and prospectors began exploring the Rocky Mountains in 1859, the fate of the Utes became all but sealed. Although the western third of Colorado had been set aside as a Ute Indian reservation, the large mineral deposits in the San Juans ensured that white men would eventually take over most of the state.

Ironically it was Ute Indian rumors that initiated the first big rush to the San Juans. Captain Charles Baker heard that gold had been discovered near present-day Silverton, and in 1860 he and six men set out to claim any promising land. Although Baker and his men discovered only small amounts of gold, the extent of their discoveries became greatly exaggerated, and many prospectors converged on the San Juans. These prospectors were largely disappointed, and after the start of the Civil War the area was abandoned.

In 1870 more gold was discovered, and prospectors once again began infiltrating the San Juans. These men were trespassing on Indian lands, and in 1872 troops were called in to keep the miners out and maintain peace. In the following year, though, the Utes were pressured into signing the Brunot Agreement, which reduced the size of their reservation by three million acres and opened the San Juans for mining.

With the Native Americns out of the picture, the path was cleared for the main "rush to the San Juans." Hundreds of miners from some of the older mining camps began moving to the area, bringing with them valuable mining experience. In short time many cabins began to spring up, and in September of 1874 Silverton was incorporated.

Although Silverton was home to many rich mines, the early days were tough, as there were few roads and no railways with which to transport supplies. This problem was eventually solved by Otto Mears who built over 400 miles of toll roads throughout the San Juans. Mears, who was known as the "Pathfinder of the San Juan," also constructed three narrow gauge railroads, called the Silverton; the Silverton, Gladstone and Northerly; and the Silverton Northern. These lines, along with the Denver & Rio Grande Railway, helped establish Silverton as the region's major railroad center.

With the improvement in transportation Silverton's economy finally began to take off. By 1882 the town had two banks, several hotels, two newspapers, three sawmills, and numerous Victorian-style buildings. In addition it was home to many saloons, dance halls, and gambling halls along the red-light district, known as Blair Street.

At one point Blair Street became so unruly that Bat Masterson was hired as sheriff to maintain order. Although Masterson did return some civility to Silverton, he never did close Blair Street, as he seemed to have enjoyed partaking in the activities along this district.

Despite the early chaos Silverton continued to prosper throughout the 1880s. Its economy relied on the mines, which poured forth vast amounts of silver. Among the more productive properties in the region were the Shenandoah-Dives, the Silver Lake, the Gold King, the Royal Tiger, and the Sunnyside.

Although Silverton thrived for many years, it barely survived the Panic of 1893. As silver prices plummeted several of the mines closed down and numerous residents left town. In short time,

though, large deposits of gold were discovered, and by 1899 Silverton had fully recovered.

Although Silverton survived the Panic of 1893, its worst days were yet to come. In 1919 the community was devastated by a terrible flu epidemic that killed over ten percent of the population. The town managed to survive, and mining continued until the beginning of World War II.

Following the war tourism replaced mining as Silverton's primary industry. Many visitors began riding the Denver & Rio Grande Narrow-Gauge Railroad, which runs from Durango to Silverton and passes through some of the finest scenery in the state.

While tourists discovered the railroad, Hollywood filmmakers discovered Blair Street, with its historic saloons and gambling halls. These old structures served as an ideal backdrop for Hollywood westerns, and over the years several motion pictures, including the *Naked Spur, Ticket to Tomahawk,* and *Around the World in Eighty Days,* were filmed in Silverton.

Today Silverton's economy remains strong. Although most of the neighboring towns have long since been abandoned, Silverton has survived through thick and thin, thus earning its nickname, "The Town that Never Quit."

In the 1880s Silverton was one of the richest mining towns in the San Juans.

Today, after surviving a century of adversity, Silverton has earned its nickname, "The Town that Never Quit."

TELLURIDE: From Mining Town to Ski

The scenic beauty and apparent calm of the small town of Telluride give no evidence of the many trials and tribulations that make up its 120-year history.

Originally established in 1878 the town was given the name Columbia. Much of the mail, however, was delivered to Columbia, California, and the name was changed to Telluride in 1881.

The mountains surrounding Telluride were home to many rich silver deposits, and numerous mines sprang up, including the Liberty Bell, Mendota, and Smuggler-Union Mines. Prosperity did not come quickly as mining supplies had to be hauled in over long distances by way of pack trains, ox teams, and freight wagons. Only with the arrival of the railroad in 1890 did transportation become more economical.

An additional hardship for Telluride resulted from its location amidst steep canyon walls. When the heavy snows fell in winter, Telluride became susceptible to snow slides. One particularly bad slide carried off all of the buildings of the Liberty Bell Mine and killed several people.

Although the early days were tough, nothing could have prepared residents for the hardships encountered in the 1890s. Following the collapse of silver prices in 1893, many of the mines closed down and the population dwindled rapidly. For a while it appeared that Telluride might not survive, but in the late 1890s numerous gold deposits were discovered and the town quickly rebounded.

With the resurgence in mining came an interest in developing a cheaper source of fuel for Telluride's mines. L. L. Nunn, a legal advisor for the Gold King Mine, approached George Westinghouse about the possibility of using alternating current to operate the mines. Westinghouse, who had been working with Nikola Tesla, the inventor of alternating current, gladly accepted Nunn's offer. He built a dam atop the cascades of the South Fork of the San Miguel River, and Nunn built a power plant in the valley below the cascades. A wire was then strung over the mountain to Telluride to supply electricity to the town and its mines. This was the first successful application of alternating current, and it paved the way for a revolutionary new method of power distribution throughout the United States.

With the mines now pouring out large amounts of gold and with this new, cheaper source of energy, Telluride finally got its first taste of prosperity. At its peak in the late 1890s, Telluride was home to twenty-six saloons and eight prostitution houses. This prosperity, however, was short-lived.

Town

At the turn of the century a long and bloody labor battle was waged between the mineworkers and the mine owners. In 1901 the union miners, belonging to the Western Federation of Miners, went on strike, demanding shorter work-hours and higher wages. They eventually won the right to an eight-hour work day, but only after much violence and several murders.

Just two years later, in 1903, the mill workers went on strike, and they were soon joined by the union miners. The mine owners appealed to Governor James H. Peabody to maintain order, and on November 20, 1903, Peabody sent 500 National Guardsmen to Telluride. The Guardsmen deported many of the strikers, and the mines were reopened with non-union workers.

Once Telluride was secured the National Guard withdrew, and control was turned over to Buckeley Wells, a mine manager and former army captain. Wells deported many union sympathizers and ransacked their houses. The Western Federation of Miners responded by arming the strikers and training them in warfare. Peabody was thus forced to recall the National Guard and impose martial law. The National Guard returned some order to Telluride, and after fourteen months of conflict a compromise was finally reached, with the real victory going to the mine owners.

Following this long and bitter strike mining in Telluride never did fully recover. Many mines began closing down in the 1920s, and by mid-century there was very little mining activity in Telluride. Although there was a momentary resurgence in the 1960s, mining finally gave way to skiing in the late 1970s.

Many of the long-time residents were reluctant to allow skiing and tourism to infiltrate Telluride. Elvira Wunderlich, a resident of Telluride since 1914, said, "Skiing does furnish a lot of jobs and supports our economy, but I liked the mining days better. A lot of our old friends are gone, and this is now a young person's town."

Although mining has come to an end in Telluride, it is by no means forgotten. Many of the mines are now being cleaned up by the Environmental Protection Agency, as even today they pose a threat to the environment. It is interesting that as yesterday's ecological hazards are being repaired, new hazards are arising in the form of skiing and tourism. Only time will tell how Telluride deals with the issue of preserving its scenic beauty amidst a growing population and rapid development.

*I*n the 1880s Telluride was a bustling mining town.

*T*oday Telluride has become a prosperous ski town.

*V*iew of Mystic Falls, near Ames, in the 1880s. A dam above the falls helped provide electricity for Telluride's mines.

C H A P T E R V : T H E S A N J U A N S

Although the rushing water has eroded some of the rocks, the secluded Mystic Falls looks much the same as it did a century ago.

LAKE CITY: Site of the Packer Massacre

On February 9, 1874, Alferd Packer and five men set out for the San Juan Mountains, hoping to lay claim to some rich silver-mining property. No one knows exactly what happened over the next sixty-five days, but it is assumed that the party got caught in a terrible snowstorm near present-day Lake City and, in desperation, Alferd Packer killed his companions and consumed their flesh.

Packer was eventually found guilty of premeditated murder and sentenced to die on May 19, 1883. He was later granted a stay of execution and spent the next eighteen years in prison. Until his death in 1906 Packer denied having killed his five companions.

Despite such inauspicious beginnings the town of Lake City went on to become a prosperous mining town. The first mineral deposits were discovered in November of 1874,

and by the fall of 1875 Lake City had 400 residents, 67 buildings, and its first newspaper, called the *Silver World*.

As with several other mining towns, Lake City's early days were characterized by crime and lawlessness. Although the town was home to many families and four churches, it was also home to Hell's Acre, a haven for thieves, gamblers, con-men, prostitutes, and murderers.

In 1882 George Betts and James W. Browning, who owned a dance hall in Hell's Acre, shot and killed Lake City Sheriff E.N. Campbell. They were later apprehended by armed scouts and then lynched by a mob of angry citizens.

Opposing the darker elements of Lake City was the Reverend George M. Darley, who preached to anyone who would listen. Darley vehemently opposed drinking and gambling and convinced numerous miners to sign temperance pledges. With his help the law-abiding citizens of Lake City were able to gain the upper hand over the lawless inhabitants of Hell's Acre.

As Lake City began to settle down, residents looked forward to more peaceful and prosperous times. However, in 1882, the Denver and Rio Grande Railroad dropped plans to extend its line to Lake City, and in the following year the Ute and Ulay Mines closed, causing a full-scale economic depression. Lake City did not begin to recover until 1887 when the mines were reopened and some new discoveries were made.

Lake City received another boost in 1889 when the Denver and Rio Grande finally arrived in town. By 1890 twenty mines were in operation and the Ute and Ulay Mines produced over $400,000 in silver. Even the Panic of 1893 did little to slow the economy. Although silver prices plummeted, Lake City compensated by

producing more gold and lead, and in 1895 the mines yielded over $700,000 worth of minerals.

Lake City finally began to decline near the turn of the century. Around this time gold production began to drop off, and many of the mines closed down. The population fell to 1,609 in 1900 and to 646 by 1910. Although mining did continue around Lake City, it was only on a limited scale. By 1970 the only mineral production was that of sand and gravel.

Today Lake City relies on tourism to support its economy. In the summer people come from all over the nation to fish, hunt, camp, and hike, and during the winter snowmobilers come to traverse the frozen landscape. If you should pass through, take time to admire the impressive scenery that surrounds this small Colorado town.

◄►

*I*n the 1880s Lake City was a prosperous,
but wild, mining town.

*T*oday Lake City is a quiet,
residential community that relies on
a strong tourist industry.

ANIMAS FORKS: From Mining Town to Ghost Town

At an elevation of 11,584 feet, Animas Forks once claimed to be "the largest town in the world (at such high an elevation)." And this it may have been, for in few places have so many hardy, or perhaps foolish, men and women resided in such inhospitable conditions.

The early residents of Animas Forks were drawn by the lure of rich mineral deposits. The first strike was made in 1875, and by 1876 there were thirty cabins, two mills, a hotel, a saloon, a general store, and a population of about 200 people. The town was incorporated in 1877, at which time one estimate had the population at 1,000.

The population figures actually refer to the summer population, as most of the residents left Animas Forks during the winter. Those who remained endured snowdrifts exceeding twenty feet and were in constant danger of the avalanches that came roaring down the precipitous mountain slopes. Many are said to have spent their time playing poker in a local saloon while waiting for the storms to pass.

When the snows finally did recede in the summer, attention again turned to the mines.

Among the more productive properties in the region were the Iron Cap, the Red Cloud, the Black Cross, the Big Giant, and the enormous Gold Prince.

These mines allowed Animas Forks to prosper well into the 1880s. As with many other mining towns, Animas Forks began to decline in the 1890s. Even the arrival of the Silverton-Northern Railroad from Eureka could not rejuvenate the economy.

Animas Forks did experience one last boom from 1904 to 1916 following the construction of the huge Gold Prince Mill. In 1917 this mill was disassembled and moved to Eureka, and Animas Forks soon joined the long list of Colorado ghost towns.

Today, while so many other abandoned camps have succumbed to the ravages of time, Animas Forks remains one of the best-preserved ghost towns in the state. Many of its old buildings are still standing, including one that was reportedly owned by the millionaire Thomas Walsh. These old structures can, like nothing else, offer visitors a first-hand glimpse into Colorado's historic past.

*I*n the 1880s Animas Forks was a great place for mining, but a tough place to live.

*A*lthough they cannot be seen in this photograph, many old buildings remain standing in Animas Forks.

EUREKA: Home of the Sunnyside Mine

The early prospectors in the San Juans must have lived in almost constant fear. Not only were they trespassing on Indian land, but they also had to endure the harsh Rocky Mountain winters with only the crudest of shelters. So you can imagine their excitement when in the 1860s they discovered gold along Animas Creek. They surely believed that all of their efforts had paid off, and thus gave the entire area the name Eureka, a Greek word meaning, "I have found it!"

Unfortunately for the early prospectors only small amounts of gold were panned, and the area was soon abandoned. The name Eureka, however, proved prophetic for the Sunnyside Mine, where silver was discovered in 1873. Sunnyside went on to become one of the state's great silver producers.

One of the early owners of the Sunnyside was John Terry, who poured most of his money into its development. Unfortunately the mine was slow to pay off, and Terry was forced to sell the mine to a New York syndicate for $75,000 and a promised $225,000 in future installments.

After spending thousands of dollars in developing the property, the syndicate became frustrated with the whole endeavor and, in lieu of the future payments, it returned the mine to Terry.

With his new funds Terry was able to aggressively develop the mine. He was soon rewarded handsomely.

As the fortunes of the Sunnyside Mine improved, so did the fortunes of Eureka. This town was established in the early 1870s, and within a few years it had several stores, a restaurant, a saloon, a mill, a post office, and a population of approximately 2,000 people.

Like many other mining towns, Eureka oftentimes found itself at the mercy of Mother Nature. The town was located at the bottom of steep mountain slopes and was subject to numerous rockslides and avalanches. One particularly bad snow slide in 1906 carried off the Silver Wing bunkhouse and killed one miner.

Despite the natural hazards Eureka continued to thrive well into the twentieth century. The economy was dependent on the Sunnyside Mine, which operated continuously until 1931, when it closed temporarily.

Following this closure Eureka's population dwindled rapidly, and the town struggled to survive. In 1937 the Sunnyside was reopened and the mill was reconditioned. In August of that year the town government was re-established and Eureka appeared to be on the rebound. Unfortunately this resurgence was short lived, for in 1939 the population began to decline, and the post office was shut down. Finally during World War II both the mine and the mill were closed, and Eureka, for all intents and purposes, closed with them.

*V*iew of
Eureka in the
1880s shows
several small
cabins in the
background.

*T*oday the
cabins are
gone and a
small road
runs through
the center of
the valley.

Thanks to the great Sunnyside Mine, Eureka, shown in the 1880s, thrived well into the twentieth century.

CHAPTER V: THE SAN JUANS

The same scene in Eureka in 1998 shows a small campground where the town site used to lie.

CHATTANOOGA: Mining Town and Transportation Center

The town of Chattanooga was established after silver deposits were discovered in the region in the late 1870s. Initially the economy was slow to take off, as the ore had to be shipped nearly 200 miles by wagon to the nearest railroad. Nevertheless there were some productive mines in the region, including the rich Silver Crown Mines.

In addition to the silver mines Chattanooga also benefited from its favorable location between the bustling towns of Silverton and Ouray. Wagons from Silverton stopped at Chattanooga, and the supplies were loaded onto pack trains for the trip over the pass to Ouray.

Although Chattanooga did experience some prosperity in the 1880s, it was hit hard by the repeal of the Sherman Act in 1893. As silver prices plummeted, many miners left town and Chattanooga struggled to survive. Fortunately, gold was soon discovered in the Hoosier Bay Mine, and the town quickly recovered.

Following this discovery the *Silverton Standard* proudly proclaimed, "Excitement is at a fever heat — all are confident that Cripple Creek cannot show anything like it." Regrettably this prognosis proved far too optimistic, and the gold quickly played out.

To make matters worse a devastating fire swept through Chattanooga in the early 1890s. Later a huge snow slide destroyed what was left of the town, leaving only the shattered remnants of many now-forgotten buildings.

*I*n the 1880s Chattanooga was busy as both a mining town and transportation center.

*T*oday Chattanooga is only a memory.

RED MOUNTAIN TOWN: From Mining Camp to Cleanup Site

Located atop a high mountain pass at an elevation of 11,300 feet, Red Mountain Town was one of the most inhospitable places to live in all of Colorado. Although silver was discovered here in 1879, only the hardiest of prospectors made their way up the pass to stake a claim.

Red Mountain finally began to take off in 1883, when Otto Mears completed a toll road from Silverton to Ouray. Many prospectors headed up the pass, and soon the town had two newspapers, a water works, a school, and numerous saloons and gambling halls.

As it continued to grow Red Mountain emerged as the largest and wealthiest town in the district. Its economy relied on the Yankee Girl, National Belle, Congress, Summit, and Enterprise Mines, and it was also aided by the construction of the Silverton Railroad over Red Mountain Pass in September of 1888.

While Red Mountain Town thrived throughout the 1880s, it was nearly obliterated by a fire in 1892. Although many of the structures were rebuilt, the Panic of 1893 ended any hopes of a revival. By 1896 the population had fallen to forty, and the future did not appear promising.

There was a momentary resurgence in 1901, when many of the mines were consolidated and the old veins were reworked. Unfortunately this effort proved short-lived, and Red Mountain Town was soon abandoned.

In 1938 a fire destroyed much of what remained of Red Mountain Town. Today there are only a few old structures to remind visitors of the days gone by. Another reminder comes in the form of the Environmental Protection Agency, which is now cleaning up many of the old mines around Red Mountain, Ironton, and Guston.

◀▶

*V*iew of Red Mountain Town in the 1880s shows several of the towns buildings.

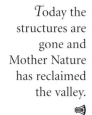

*T*oday the structures are gone and Mother Nature has reclaimed the valley.

*R*ed Mountain Town, shown in the 1880s, was a prosperous mining camp.

CHAPTER V: THE SAN JUANS

*R*ed Mountain in 1998 is a remnant of its former self. It is now being cleaned up by the Environmental Protection Agency.

CHAPTER VI
SOUTH-CENTRAL
COLORADO

DEL NORTE: Gateway to the San Juan

For hundreds of years the area around present-day Del Norte was inhabited by the Ute Indians. The Utes lived in relative isolation until the mid-1600s, when several Spanish explorers, including General Don Diego de Vargas and Governor Juan Bautista de Anza, began infiltrating the region.

Another notable visitor to the area was John C. Fremont, who arrived in the San Luis Valley during the winter of 1848-49. Fremont's party was ill-prepared for the cold weather and heavy snow, and eleven members of the group died in the area around present-day Del Norte.

Approximately ten years after this tragedy, a group of fourteen New Mexican families arrived in the San Luis Valley and established the first permanent settlement in the region. In later years many other Spanish immigrants came to the region and established settlements throughout the San Luis Valley.

While Spanish settlers continued to migrate to the valley, the Americans largely ignored the area. This began to change in 1870 following the discovery of gold in the San Juan Mountains and in Summitville. These discoveries attracted thousands of prospectors to the region, and in 1871 Del Norte was established as a supply town to the many up-and-coming mining camps.

Early on Del Norte was a rather wild and uncivilized community. The town had many saloons and dance halls, and several murders, stage robberies, prison escapes, and lynchings are said to have taken place here.

In contrast to these unruly elements, the town also had some of the cultural necessities, including a school, a library, and an opera house. Also in 1883 the Presbyterian College of the Southwest, which served as both a church and a college, was established in Del Norte.

By the early 1880s the San Juan region had become so prosperous that millionaire Thomas Bowen proposed creating a new state, called "San Juan." This proposal, which would have established Del Norte as the state capital, is said to have lost by just one vote.

Although Del Norte lost its chance to become capital, it nevertheless continued to grow and prosper. In addition to its status as a supply town, it also became a ranching and farming community. These industries helped Del Norte survive the Panic of 1893, even as many of the mining camps were abandoned.

Throughout the twentieth century Del Norte's economy remained strong. Events of note during this time include the construction of the Rio Grande County Courthouse in 1942 and the introduction of beer brewing barley as a crop in the 1950s.

Today, while Del Norte continues to rely on ranching and farming, it is also aided by the tourist and lumber industries. In addition several of the town's residents are employed by the Environmental Protection Agency, as part of the Superfund Cleanup site located twenty-six miles away in Summitville.

*D*el Norte, shown in the 1880s, was known as "The Gateway to the San Juan."

*D*el Norte, shown in 1998, continues to grow and prosper, thanks in part to its ranching and farming industries.

SUMMITVILLE: From Mining Town to

If you come to Summitville today, you may think that the mines are still active. Dozens of workers are busy throughout the day, and the entire area is being dug up, giving the former town site the appearance more of a moonscape than a lush mountain valley. The workers here, however, are doing anything but mining. They are employed by the Environmental Protection Agency and are working on one of the latest Superfund sites. This project, which began in 1993, has cost taxpayers hundreds of millions of dollars and may not be completed for several more years.

The early prospectors in Summitville certainly had little idea that it would take many years and millions of dollars to repair the damage that mining would inflict on the landscape. They were simply trying to strike it rich at a time when mining-fever had enveloped the state.

The first discovery in the region was made by James and William Wightman, who struck gold on South Mountain in 1870. Although this find drew some prospectors to the area, the town really took off in 1873 when the Little Annie Mine was discovered. This mine, which would go on to become the largest gold producer in Summitville, helped make the former judge and future senator, Thomas Bowen, a millionaire.

In addition to the Little Annie, several other rich mines were discovered along South Mountain, and by the early 1880s Summitville had become the largest camp in the district. The town had nine mills, fourteen saloons, a

Superfund Site

newspaper, and a population of approximately 600 people.

As soon as Summitville reached its peak, it began to decline. Many of the best mines appeared to be depleted, and numerous residents left town. By 1889 the population had fallen to twenty-five, and by 1893 the town was deserted.

Although residents had given up on Summitville, there was still plenty of gold to be mined. In 1934 the Summitville Consolidated Mines, Inc., began reworking many of the old mines, and by 1935 Summitville had become the second largest mining camp in the state.

Although this boom brought much wealth to the region, it came to an abrupt end at the beginning of World War II, when all non-essential

mining was banned by the federal government. The only mining that continued in Summitville was that of copper.

Following the war the Summitville Consolidated Mining Company continued mining operations in Summitville. In 1986 the company began mining some of the lower-grade silver and gold using an open-pit mining operation. The acid runoff from this mine began leaking into the Alamosa River, which irrigates much of the farmland in the San Luis Valley. As a result the mine was shut down in 1992, and shortly thereafter the Environmental Protection Agency began work on the massive Superfund project that is taking place there today.

*I*n the early 1880s Summitville was one of the state's leading gold producers.

CHAPTER VI: SOUTH-CENTRAL COLORADO

Today Summitville is a Super Fund clean-up site. Due to restricted access to the area, exact duplication of the historic photo was impossible.

ROSITA: The Little Rose

According to legend the town of Rosita was named by a Frenchman whose Spanish lover had died in Mexico City. Following her death the Frenchman became very distraught and wandered aimlessly all the way to Colorado. He eventually arrived at a small town in the Wet Mountain Valley near the base of the Sangre de Cristo Mountain Range. He found the area to be nearly as beautiful as his lost love, and thus named it Rosita, in her honor.

This story, however fanciful, is probably untrue. The town is generally believed to have been named by Dick Irwin, who called it Rosita — meaning 'Little Rose' — because of the abundance of wild roses in the area.

Irwin was one of three prospectors who located rich mineral deposits in the region in 1873. In the following year the Hamboldt and Pocahontas Mines were discovered, and the town began to take off.

Within a couple of years Rosita had 2,000 residents, a newspaper, two reduction works, a smelter, four churches, two hotels, a brewery, and a cheese factory. The cheese factory was once the largest in the state, and it was worked until the cows reportedly began eating too much wild garlic, thus contaminating the milk.

As Rosita continued to grow it experienced some of the crime and lawlessness that was common in the early mining camps. One story relates that printed invitations were sent out inviting people to a "Necktie Party" prior to the lynching of two suspected murderers.

Another story asserts that a man named Major Graham came to Rosita and illegally took control of the Pocahontas Mine. The residents of Rosita refused to allow this sort of lawlessness and eventually reclaimed control of the mine during a fierce gunfight.

Although Rosita's peak years were certainly eventful, they were also very fleeting. In 1878 many residents left Rosita and headed to the boom town of Silver Cliff. Any hope of a revival was wiped out in 1881, when a devastating fire swept through town. Although some of

the buildings were rebuilt, Rosita never fully recovered.

For several decades following this fire, Rosita lingered on the brink of oblivion. The town finally began to recover in the 1950s when the Metro-Goldwyn-Mayer company came to Rosita and shot the western movie *Saddle in the Wind*. Although area residents had dreams of establishing Rosita as a major motion picture location, no other movie was ever filmed in town.

Today little is left of Rosita. Although a few houses remain scattered throughout the valley, the town's peak years are a distant memory.

*R*osita, shown in the 1880s, was a prosperous silver mining town until larger deposits were discovered in the neighboring town of Silver Cliff.

*T*oday only a few houses are scattered throughout Rosita.

QUERIDA: Site of the Bassick Mine

In 1877 E.C. Bassick discovered silver deposits in an old prospect hole near present-day Querida. Following this discovery Bassick quit his job with the Centennial Mining Company and staked a claim.

The first carload of ore from the Bassick Mine was valued at $10,000. Over the next eighteen months Bassick mined another $500,000 in silver and gold from the property. He then sold the mine to an eastern syndicate for $500,000 and a ten percent stake in the new company.

The town that emerged around the Bassick Mine was initially called Bassickville. Later in 1879 David Livingstone changed the name to Querida. Livingstone, who was one of the town's founders, chose this name — meaning 'beloved' or 'darling' in Spanish — because he is said to have fallen in love with the area.

Querida grew rapidly at first, and it soon had a post office, a few stores, a hotel, a saw mill, a smelting works, and a population of 500. This growth came to an abrupt end in 1884, when the Bassick Mine became tied up in litigation. For the next fifteen years the mine was worked intermittently, before ownership finally reverted to Bassick's heirs.

In 1903 the Melrose Gold Mining Company purchased most of the mining claims and built a cyanide reduction plant and an electric light plant on the property. Just one year later the company discovered a gold lode worth approximately $2 million. Following this discovery mining began to decline, and in the late 1920s Querida was abandoned.

Querida, shown in the 1880s, was established after E.C. Bassick discovered the rich Bassick Mine.

Today Querida is abandoned and little evidence remains of the former town site.

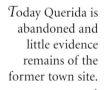

SILVER CLIFF: The County Seat of Custer

In the late 1870s R.J. Edwards, Robert Powell, and George Hofford discovered deposits of horn silver near present-day Silver Cliff. When word of their discovery reached the neighboring towns of Rosita and Querida, a large group of prospectors rushed to the area. These prospectors were largely disappointed, and most of them quickly returned home. Edwards, Powell, and Hofford, though, did not give up so easily, and they soon discovered silver at 740 ounces to the ton.

Following this discovery a second, and larger, group of prospectors converged on the area. In short time several buildings were constructed, and on December 8, 1879, Silver Cliff was incorporated. The new town grew rapidly, and by 1880 it had a population of approximately 5,000 people.

Early on Silver Cliff was described as a wild and unruly community. The first women to arrive were all prostitutes, and the town had twenty-five saloons, all of which were packed nearly every day of the week.

As it continued to grow Silver Cliff began to settle down. Many churches, of all different faiths, were constructed, and schools followed shortly thereafter. The town also had twenty grocery stores, two banks, ten hotels, two smelters, and several newspapers.

Although the early days were prosperous, they were not without their difficulties. In 1880 a devastating fire swept through Silver Cliff, destroying many of the buildings. Just two

County

years later, after Silver Cliff had been partially rebuilt, another fire broke out in the main business district. On this occasion the firefighters were able to get the upper hand, and the fire was extinguished before it could do much damage.

Another problem for Silver Cliff arose from a dispute between the Bull and Domingo Mines. These mines were working from the same silver vein, and a controversy soon arose between the respective owners. Eventually the case went to court, and the Bull gained an order banning the Domingo group from their own mine. The Domingo miners refused to leave and tensions quickly escalated. After a few brief confrontations both sides finally agreed to sell their property to an eastern

syndicate, which then merged the two mines.

Despite the early difficulties Silver Cliff continued to grow and prosper throughout the 1880s. By 1881 it had become the third largest town in Colorado, and in 1886 it replaced Rosita as the county seat of Custer County.

Not long after capturing the county seat, Silver Cliff began to decline. The town was devastated by the Panic of 1893, and for several years it lingered on the brink of oblivion. Somehow Silver Cliff managed to recover and it has survived to the present day. Although it is no longer a large and boisterous community, Silver Cliff can nevertheless claim to have endured the turbulent mining days while many other towns did not.

*I*n the 1880s Silver Cliff was one of the largest towns in Colorado.

*Un*like many neighboring mining towns, Silver Cliff has survived to the present day.

MANITOU SPRINGS: The Saratoga of the

Prior to the arrival of the white man, the Cheyenne, Arapaho, and Ute Indians all frequented the hot springs at Manitou. These springs were considered a sacred place and were used as a neutral location for warriors to recuperate during war.

The first American to view the hot springs was Stephen H. Long, who passed through the area during his historic expedition in 1820. One member of Long's party, Dr. Edwin James, was very impressed by the springs and wrote, "The water is beautifully transparent, has a sparkling appearance, the grateful taste and exhilarating effect of the most highly aerated artificial mineral water."

The first permanent settler near the springs was Richens Wootton, who claimed 160 acres of land and constructed a log cabin in 1859. This property later changed hands several times, before being purchased by General William Jackson Palmer in 1871. Palmer had dreams of converting the area into a grand resort center, and he quickly laid out the town of La Font, which would later be renamed Manitou.

After founding the town Palmer constructed an elegant hotel called the Manitou House. This hotel had fifty-eight rooms, two lakes, and a fountain, and it attracted tourists from all over the world. In later years several other hotels were built in Manitou, and the town emerged as a prominent resort center.

In addition to tourism Manitou also had a temporary mining boom. In December of 1875 the Ute Pass Lode was discovered, and many prospectors rushed to the area. By April of 1876 the gold had played out and the miners moved on.

Fortunately Manitou never relied too heavily on mining. Throughout the late 1870s tourists continued to flock to Manitou, and by 1881 the town had become known as the "Saratoga of the West." Among the early visitors to Manitou was Ulysses S. Grant, who stayed for one night at the Manitou House in 1875 and for a month at the Beebe House in 1880. In later years both President McKinley and Thomas Edison also came to Manitou.

The tourists at Manitou were attracted not only to the hot springs, but they were also

West

drawn to the many nearby scenic attractions. The most popular destination was Pikes Peak, which looms impressively above Manitou Springs. In 1888 the Pikes Peak Carriage Road was constructed to the top of Pikes Peak, and in 1891 a railway called Cog Road arrived at the summit.

Another popular attraction was the Cave of the Winds which was discovered by Arthur Love in 1871. In later years several more caves, all of which were part of the same formation, were discovered in the vicinity.

Other attractions near Manitou Springs included the Garden of the Gods, Seven Falls, Rainbow Falls, Cheyenne Mountain, Monument Park, Crystal Park, and Seven Lakes. These scenic wonders have drawn ever-increasing numbers of tourists and have allowed Manitou Springs to grow and prosper throughout the twentieth century.

Today the many sight-seeing opportunities near Manitou Springs may overwhelm many of the visitors. An unknown writer for the *Gazette* in 1907 summed up this predicament well:

The tourist sat by the Manitou Spring,
His legs were stiff and sore,
Still proudly he flourished his Alpine staff
As he counted his exploits o'er.

"I've finished the canons now," he said.
"And I've climbed the Seven Falls;
I've been to the grave of Helen Hunt,
Where the lonely blue-bird calls."

"I walked to the Peak last night," he sighed;
"Tomorrow I climb Cheyenne;
I'll spend today at Monument Park,
(I've been but I'm going again.)"

"And then I must go to the Seven Lakes,
And I've got to do Crystal Park;
Next day I'm going to Cripple Creek
To examine the gold mines dark."

The tourist that sat by the Manitou spring
Was merry and blythe and gay;
But he over-exerted himself that week,
And the next, they laid him away!

The box reached home with the tourist dead,
They wept, and they wept again,
Till the tourist rose with a fearful shriek,
"Wait, I forgot to do North Cheyenne!"
(Daniels, *The Springs of Manitou*)

*M*anitou Springs was a prominent resort town in the 1880s.

Today, thanks to the many scenic attractions, Manitou Springs remains a popular tourist destination.

View of Manitou Springs in the 1880s with Pikes Peak in the distance.

The same view of Manitou Springs in 1997 shows some additional development and a new growth of trees in the valley.

*I*n the 1880s Rainbow Falls was a popular and pristine tourist destination.

*T*oday Rainbow Falls lies near an overpass that is covered with graffiti.

Seven Falls was a popular scenic attraction in the 1880s.

CHAPTER VI: SOUTH-CENTRAL COLORADO

Today Seven Falls remains one of the region's finest scenic wonders.

CHAPTER VII
THE FRONT RANGE

DENVER: The Queen City

In the summer of 1858 the Russell Party arrived in the present-day Colorado area and began prospecting for gold at the base of the Rocky Mountains. After several tiresome weeks they finally discovered small deposits of gold near the present-day Denver. When these deposits played out, the party headed north to Wyoming. In the fall they returned to Colorado, and on November 1, 1858, they established the town of Auraria.

Meanwhile, on the other side of Cherry Creek, another group called the Lawrence Party staked a claim and established the St. Charles Town Company. In the fall of 1858 the party returned east to obtain a charter for the new town. They left one man, Charles Nichols, to protect their claim.

While the Lawrence Party was gone, another group known as the Leavenworth Party arrived in Colorado and camped in Auraria. They later moved to the Lawrence claim, and on November 17, 1858, they staked a claim of their own. When Nichols protested they threatened to lynch him, and he quickly backed down.

On November 22, 1858, the Leavenworth Party formed the Denver City Town Company. E.P. Stout was elected president, and William Larimer became the secretary and donating agent. The town was named after the former governor of the Kansas Territory, James Denver, who unbeknownst to them had resigned three weeks earlier.

Early on Denver City's economy was aided by the gold discoveries made by George Jackson and John Gregory near Idaho Springs and Central City. When word of these discoveries leaked out a large rush of prospectors headed to the mountains, and Denver City soon emerged as a major supply town to the mining camps. By June of 1859 Denver City had over 100 cabins and the town of Auraria had approximately 250 cabins. In April of 1860 these two communities and another camp called Highland merged into one town called Denver.

Although Denver grew rapidly at first, it struggled throughout much of the 1860s. During this time the entire state was hampered by the struggling hard-rock mining industry, which did not have the proper capital or financing to effectively mine the lower-grade ores. As a result Denver's population grew from 4,749 in 1860 to just 4,759 in 1870.

Denver was hurt not only by the mining difficulties, but it was also hit by a pair of natural disasters. On April 19, 1863, a fire swept through town, destroying many of the buildings. Just over one year later, on May 20, 1864, heavy rains caused the Cherry Creek and South Platte Rivers to rise above their banks, and much of the town was flooded. Among the buildings destroyed were the Methodist Church, the City Hall, and the *Rocky Mountain News* building.

Despite the early difficulties Denver remained the most prominent town in Colorado, and in 1867 it was elected the capital of Colorado Territory replacing the town of Golden.

Denver received another boost following the arrival of the transcontinental railroad in Cheyenne, Wyoming, in 1868. Although many had expected the line to run through Denver, residents quickly raised funds for the establishment of the Denver Pacific Railroad. In June of 1870 this company completed a spur line to Cheyenne, and Denver's economy finally began to take off.

In addition to the railroad Denver also benefited from the construction of the Argo Smelter in 1878. In the following years several more mills and smelters were constructed throughout town, and Denver became known as the "Smelting Capital of the Rockies."

As a result of this activity Denver's population grew from less than 5,000 in 1870 to approximately 35,000 in 1880. With all of this growth came the same type of crime and lawlessness that was prevalent throughout the West. Much of this violence occurred along three blocks of McGaa Street known as "the Row." This area had many saloons and gambling halls, and it remained the red-light district until 1915 when many of the establishments were closed down.

Despite the early chaos Denver continued to grow and prosper throughout the 1880s. In 1881 it became the state capital, and five years later work began on the capitol building. In addition many other buildings including the Tabor Grand Opera House, the Windsor Hotel, Union Station, the Arapahoe County Courthouse, and the Brown Palace Hotel were constructed.

Denver's rapid economic growth finally came to an end following the repeal of the Sherman Act in 1893. As silver prices plummeted numerous mines closed down, and thousands of prospectors descended on Denver. Few of these men could find jobs, and the number of unemployed quickly reached into the thousands.

As the economy continued to deteriorate, many businesses were forced to close down. Among the hardest hit were the banks and savings institutions. In mid-July there were several bank runs throughout Denver, and three banks went out of business in just ten days.

During these difficult times the economy was supported to some extent by the rich gold discoveries in Cripple Creek. These discoveries created a new group of millionaires in Colorado, and several of these men, including the "Midas of the West," W.S. Stratton, came to Denver to invest some of their money.

Although these individuals helped the community recover, Denver still remained a rather crude and barren town. This began to change in 1904 when Robert Speer was elected mayor. After taking office Speer enacted the "City Beautiful" campaign and began orchestrating several new projects around Denver. Amongst these projects was the construction of the Civic Center, the completion of Speer Boulevard, and the establishment of 262 miles of sewers. Speer was also instrumental in the creation of several new parks and in the planting of many new trees throughout Denver. Due in part to his contributions, Denver's population grew from 133,859 in 1900 to 256,369 in 1920.

The next influential mayor was Benjamin Stapleton who was elected in 1923. At the time of his election Stapleton was a member of the Ku Klux Klan. This group had become very powerful in Denver, and it organized many marches, rallies, and cross burnings throughout town. In later years the Klan began to decline, and Stapleton came to oppose the group.

Stapleton's most notable contribution as mayor was the construction of the Denver Municipal Airport in 1929. Initially many people opposed this airport and referred to it as "Stapleton's Folly." In later years, though, the airport proved to be well worth the investment, and in 1944 it was renamed Stapleton Airport in honor of the mayor.

Shortly after the completion of the airport, Colorado and the nation plunged into depression. By 1933 the unemployment rate in Denver had reached twenty-five percent, and the homeless population increased on a daily basis.

Colorado residents received some support from the federal government at the beginning of the New Deal in 1933. Between March 9 and June 16 Franklin Delano Roosevelt enacted many new federal programs designed to provide jobs for the masses of unemployed workers. Some of these programs, which became known as the alphabet soup, included the Federal Emergency Relief Administration (FERA), the Civil Works Administration (CWA), the Public Works Administration (PWA), and the Works Progress Administration (WPA).

Although these programs gave relief to some residents, the Depression nevertheless dragged on through the 1930s. Only with the beginning of World War II did the economy begin to recover. During the war several military installations, including the Denver Ordnance Plant, the Rocky Mountain Arsenal, and Buckley Field, were constructed, and Denver began to emerge as a major industrial center.

Following the war Denver's economy continued to recover. Many of the military plants were converted into government facilities, and Denver came to employ 20,000 government workers. In addition both manufacturing and tourism emerged as major industries, and by 1950 the population of metropolitan Denver had increased to 563,832.

Denver continued to grow and prosper throughout the 1950s. This growth was aided by the repeal of the twelve-story building height limitation in 1952. Following this act many high-rise structures, including several apartment complexes, were constructed across Denver. In order to make room for these buildings, many historic structures, including several of the mansions along Capitol Hill, were demolished.

With the destruction of these buildings came an interest in historic preservation. In 1963 the Larimer Square Associates was formed to help preserve the buildings between 14th & 15th Streets along Larimer Street. Later in 1967 the Denver Landmark Preservation Commission was created to identify structures as historic landmarks. Also in 1970 a private organization, called Historic Denver, was formed to save the Molly Brown House from destruction.

As a result of these efforts, a number of Denver's historic structures, including the D&F Tower, the Equitable Building, the Denver Dry Goods Building, and the Brown Palace Hotel, survive today. Unfortunately many other buildings have been destroyed.

While some of the historic structures were spared, new high-rises continued to spring up throughout Denver. Many of these buildings were constructed in the 1970s to accommodate the energy companies that came to Colorado following the oil embargo in 1973.

Although the energy companies helped support Denver's economy for several years, the town was hit by a recession in 1982. Many of the energy companies left town, and the community was also hurt by falling real estate prices and the savings and loan crisis.

Denver finally began to recover in the early 1990s. This recovery has brought about a new era of growth in Denver. Much of this growth has occurred along the Platte Valley where several new construction projects, including Coors Field, the Pepsi Center, Invesco Field, Elitch Gardens, and Colorado Ocean Journey, have been undertaken. Another impetus for growth came with the completion of Denver International Airport in 1995.

With all of this development it is difficult to imagine that only 140 years ago the Russell Party arrived at an empty valley where they made their historic gold discovery. It is even more difficult to imagine what changes will take place over the next 140 years. Although much can be conjectured, only time will tell how Denver reacts to the many challenges and obstacles that it will face in the coming years.

*V*iew of 17th & California looking northwest circa 1900 shows the California Building in the left foreground, followed by the Equitable Building. The Albany Hotel is in the right foreground.

CHAPTER VII: THE FRONT RANGE

Today many high rises have sprung up along 17th Avenue. The only historic structure that remains standing is the
Equitable Building.

View of 17th & California looking southwest circa 1900. The building in the right foreground is the
California Building; the structure in the right background is the Denver Dry Goods Building.

*Although most of
them have been
remodeled, many
historic structures
remain standing
along California
Avenue.*

*V*iew of the Denver Dry Goods Building circa 1900.

The same scene in 2000 shows modest changes. Media Play now occupies the lower level of the Dry Goods Building, while several lofts are available for rent in the upper levels.

The Brown Palace Hotel, shown in the 1890s, was one of the tallest buildings in Denver.

CHAPTER VII: THE FRONT RANGE

Today the Brown Palace is dwarfed by the many high rise structures that have been constructed along 17th Avenue.

174 LAWRENCE STREET. DENVER

View of Lawrence Street from 15th Street in the 1880s. The Denver Fur Company and Joslins Dry Goods buildings lie in the center background.

The same scene along Lawrence Street in 1997 shows the Westin Hotel in the center background.

*V*iew of
Larimer Street
from 17th Street
in the 1870s.

*T*he same scene
along Larimer
Street in 2000
appears much
different. Many of
the historic
structures were
torn down
following World
War II to make
room for new high
rise buildings.

*V*iew of 16th & Stout in the 1890s. The Steele Building is in the right foreground, followed by the Equitable Building.

The same scene in Denver in 1997 shows significant changes. Only the Equitable Building
remains standing from a century ago.

View of 15th Street in Denver shows one of the town's early trolley cars.

CHAPTER VII: THE FRONT RANGE

*T*he same scene in Denver in 1997 shows many changes from a century ago.

The Tabor Block, shown in the 1880s, was located on the Southeast corner of 16th & Larimer.

Today the Tabor Block is gone and 16th Street has changed dramatically.

The Milwaukee Brewery, shown in the 1880s, continued to operate until 1969, producing Denver Beer.

CHAPTER VII: THE FRONT RANGE

*O*ver the years the structure has been expanded, and it is now the Tivoli Building.

CHAPTER VII: THE FRONT RANGE

View of Market
Street in the 1880s.
The building on the
right, called Clark &
Gruber, was the first
mint in Denver.
Photo courtesy
Denver Public
Library.

Today
several of
the
buildings
along
Market
Street have
been
replaced by
a parking
lot.

GOLDEN: The County Seat of Jefferson

The town of Golden is nestled between the Rocky Mountains and North and South Table Mountains. It is one of the most beautiful and historic towns in all of Colorado.

The first American to visit Golden was Stephen H. Long, who camped in the area as part of the second official expedition through Colorado territory. Later in 1846 the legendary trappers Kit Carson and Louis Vasquez are believed to have passed through the region.

The first permanent group of settlers in Golden was the "Boston Company," which arrived on June 12, 1859. On June 16 this group met for the purpose of organizing a new town, and within four days Golden City was established.

Among the town's founders was W.A.H. Loveland who was instrumental in Golden's early development. He established the first store in town, constructed the first road up Clear Creek Canyon, and later established the Colorado Central Railroad.

Due in part to Loveland's contributions, Golden grew rapidly and it emerged as both a supply town and a coal and clay mining camp. By 1860 the population had reached 700, and the community had a hotel, a trading post, a school, a sawmill, a plaster mill, and the state's second newspaper, called *The Western Mountaineer*. Also in 1860 Golden was elected the county seat of Jefferson County, and in 1862 it became the capital of Colorado Territory.

Despite its status as capital, Golden remained second to Denver in both size and prominence. All but two of the legislative sessions were adjourned and then moved to Denver, and finally, during the seventh session in 1867, Denver was elected capital.

Not only did Golden lose its status as capital, but it also fell on hard times in the 1860s. Like many other towns Golden was hurt by the state's struggling hard-rock mining industry, and between 1860 and 1870 the population dropped by forty-two percent.

Golden finally began to recover in the 1870s. During this time it benefited from increased mining activity in the mountain towns, and it also emerged as an agricultural and industrial center.

Another factor in Golden's development was the arrival of the transcontinental railroad in Cheyenne, Wyoming, in 1868. In short time both

County

the Colorado Central and Denver Pacific Railroads began constructing spur lines to Cheyenne. The Denver Pacific arrived in Cheyenne before the Colorado Central, but Golden nevertheless remained an important railroad center, and in 1880 it served thirty trains daily.

In addition to the railroad Golden was also aided by the establishment of the Colorado School of Mines. The first building on campus, Jarvis Hall, was constructed in 1869. Shortly after it was completed, this structure was destroyed in a severe windstorm. It was quickly rebuilt, and it opened for classes in 1870.

Another impetus for growth came with the establishment of the Coors Brewery. This brewery was founded by Adolph Coors and Jacob Schueler in 1873, and it would go on to become the largest single-source brewery in the world.

Despite its rapid growth in the 1870s, Golden began to fall on hard times in the 1880s. Much of the business activity moved to Denver, and many of the prospectors in the nearby mining camps headed to Leadville. Nevertheless the community persevered, and Golden began to recover in the early twentieth century.

One factor in this recovery was the continued growth of the Coors Brewery. Although the company was hurt by Prohibition in 1916, it survived by producing malted milk and chemical porcelain. The porcelain plant grew rapidly and for a while it was the largest in the world.

The Colorado School of Mines also grew significantly during the twentieth century. In the 1940s many new structures, including a library and chemistry, metallurgy, petroleum, physical education, and geology buildings, were added to the campus. As a result "Mines" emerged as one of the nation's leading engineering schools.

Today Golden continues to grow and prosper. The downtown area has recently been revitalized and a new state of the art courthouse was completed in 1993. While this development should ensure a bright future for Golden, the town still has not forgotten its past. Many nineteenth century buildings remain standing, including the former state legislative building. As a result visitors can find one of the best-preserved towns in the state just fifteen miles west of Denver.

The town of Golden, shown from the northeast in the 1870s, is one of Colorado's oldest communities. The round building in the foreground is a railroad station.

CHAPTER VII: THE FRONT RANGE

Golden has undergone many changes but still retains much of the flavor of its historic past.

*V*iew of Golden in the 1870s shows Clear Creek in the foreground and South Table Mountain in the background. Photo courtesy Denver Public Library.

*T*he same scene in Golden in 1998 shows dramatic changes. Coors Brewery lies in the background.

*V*iew of 12th Street
looking towards Lookout
Mountain in the 1870s.

*T*he same scene in
Golden in 2000 shows
only modest changes.

CHAPTER VII: THE FRONT RANGE

Washington Avenue, shown
in the 1870s, was the center
of business activity in
Golden. Photo courtesy
Denver Public Library.

The same scene along Washington Avenue
in 1997 shows many of the same buildings
from a century ago.

BOULDER: Site of the University of

In October of 1858 Captain Thomas Aikens led a party of prospectors to what he described as "the loveliest of all the valleys in the scope of vision — a landscape exceedingly beautiful." It was here at the base of Boulder Canyon that Aikens and his men stopped to set up camp.

At the time the Arapaho Indians were the primary inhabitants of the region, and they are said to have distrusted the early settlers. A story relates that the Arapaho chief, Left Hand, approached Captain Aikens and told him, "Go away; you come to kill our game, to burn our wood, and to destroy our grass." Another Arapaho named Bear Head is said to have pointed up to a comet and declared, "Do you know what that star with a pointer means? The pointer points back to when the stars fell as thick as the tears of our women shall fall when you come to drive us away."

Despite the Arapahos' pleas Aikens and his men remained in the valley and constructed a dozen crude cabins along what is now Pearl Street. The party then began prospecting in the mountains above town and eventually discovered gold at present-day Gold Hill.

As word of their discovery spread, more prospectors headed to the region, and in February of 1859 the town of Boulder City was established. Since Colorado had not yet achieved territorial status, the town was incorporated as part of the Nebraska Territory.

By 1860 Boulder City had a sawmill, a post office, and the first public school house in Colorado. Its economy was dependent on the neighboring mining towns, as well as coal mining, ranching, and agriculture.

Although Boulder City grew rapidly at first, it struggled throughout much of the 1860s. The economy finally began to pick up in 1869 when rich silver discoveries were made near Caribou. As prospectors rushed to the new mining camp, Boulder emerged as a major supply town, and by 1873 it had a population of 1,000.

Another factor in Boulder's growth was the establishment of the University of Colorado. Although this institution was initially approved by the territorial legislature in 1861, construction did not begin on the first building, called Old Main, until 1875. Before it could be completed this structure was partially destroyed during a severe windstorm in February of 1876. It was, however, quickly rebuilt, and on September 5, 1877, it opened for classes.

In addition to the university several hotels and other business establishments were built in Boulder in the 1870s. Also the Boulder City Brewery, which was later renamed the Crystal Springs Brewery, was constructed in 1876. At its

Colorado

peak this brewery produced one million bottles of beer per year, and it continued to operate until the beginning of Prohibition in 1916.

Boulder was also home to several saloons, gambling halls, and dance halls. These establishments were among the wildest in the state and gave Boulder a reputation as a rather crude and uncivilized community.

Boulder finally began to settle down in 1897 when the Citizen's Reform League was established. This group passed a resolution to make Boulder the "cleanest and purest city within the state," and it worked to close down many of the saloons and dance halls.

While some of the seedier businesses were shut down other more respectable establishments, including a sanitarium and the Texas-Colorado Chautauqua, were constructed in the late nineteenth century. These businesses brought continued growth to Boulder, and in the 1890s the population increased from 3,330 to 6,150.

Throughout the early twentieth century Boulder continued to grow and prosper. Although the community was hurt by two world wars, the Great Depression, and Prohibition, Boulder persevered and the population continued to rise. During this time the economy was supported by an oil and tungsten boom, and by the emergence of farming as a major industry.

While Boulder experienced some prosperity in the early twentieth century, it really took off in the 1950s when it emerged as a major manufacturing and research center. In 1950 Boulder was selected as the site of the Central Radio Propagation Laboratory of the United States Bureau of Standards. Later in 1953 the Rocky Flats Plant was built nine miles south of Boulder to construct components of nuclear weapons. Also in 1964 work began on a laboratory and office building for the National Center for Atmospheric Research. As a result Boulder's population grew from 19,999 in 1950 to 37,718 in 1960.

With all of this growth residents became concerned that Boulder was being overrun too rapidly by excessive development. In order to protect the town's natural landscape, voters approved the Danish Plan in 1976. This plan restricted the number of building permits that could be issued by the city and brought an abrupt end to Boulder's rapid growth.

In addition to the Danish Plan, Boulder residents also worked to purchase open space and revitalize the downtown area. These efforts have helped preserve the town's scenic beauty, and as a result Boulder can still claim to be "the loveliest of all the valleys in the scope of vision."

❧

Early view of Boulder City, looking across Boulder Creek at the Flatirons, shows a pristine landscape.

*A*lthough Boulder has changed dramatically over the years, the community has taken measures to preserve its natural landscape.

*B*oulder Falls, shown in the 1870s, was one of the finest scenic attractions in the Boulder area. Photo courtesy Denver Public Library.

CHAPTER VII: THE FRONT RANGE

*T*oday Boulder Falls remains a popular tourist destination.

GREELEY: The Union Colony

In 1869 Nathan C. Meeker, who worked as an agriculture columnist for the *New York Tribune,* conceived of establishing a farming colony in the West. With permission from his boss, Horace Greeley, Meeker promoted the colony in the *Tribune* and he soon received over 3,000 responses.

On December 23, 1869, a meeting was held at the Cooper Institute for the purpose of organizing the colony. During this meeting, which was chaired by Horace Greeley, 438 people joined the "Union Colony." Later 297 more would join giving a total of 735.

On February 13, 1870, a locating committee consisting of Meeker, Robert Cameron, and A.C. Fisk set out to find a suitable location for the colony. These men eventually settled on the valley of the Cache la Poudre in Colorado. With the help of William N. Byers they acquired 9,324 acres of land from the railroad company, 2,592 acres from private individuals, and filed a claim for an additional 60,000 acres.

On April 20, 1870, the board of trustees met to establish the by-laws of the community. Since the members of the colony were all of "good character" and very religious, the laws were fairly strict. They did not allow any saloons, dance halls, or other "objectionable activities," and they prohibited the manufacture and sale of alcohol.

The first colony members began arriving in April and May. Each settler was entitled to a parcel of land outside the town and was given the opportunity to purchase a town lot for $25 to $50. The proceeds raised by this sale were to be used for the construction of a schoolhouse, a town hall, and other improvements "for the common good."

Since there were no houses in town, H.T. West, who had joined the locating committee in Chicago, quickly erected a large wooden building which he called the Hotel de Comfort. This "hotel" was a rather crude structure, and residents stayed only as long as they needed to build a house or a tent.

One of the first orders of business in the new colony was the construction of ditches to irrigate the farmland. Although four ditches were initially planned, only two were built using colony funds. The other ditches, now known as the Larimer & Weld Canal and the Greeley & Loveland Canal, were constructed in later years by private individuals.

In addition to the irrigation ditches colony members also began constructing some of the town's essential buildings. A town hall and a few churches were built with colony funds, and other buildings, such as a library, a farmer's club, and the dramatic association were established by individual members. Also in 1873 the impressive Meeker School Building was built at a cost of $25,000.

As Greeley continued to grow it quickly emerged as one of the most influential towns in the region. By the mid-1880s it had several churches, the Oasis Hotel, a post office, three banks, four tanneries, two newspapers, an opera house, and the second electric light plant in Colorado, called the Greeley Electric Light Company. It was also home to the Barnum House and the Barnum Block which were built by P.T. Barnum.

Although these early businesses helped diversify the economy, Greeley remained largely dependent on agriculture. The early residents struggled against many odds to grow their crops along what had become known as "The Great American Desert." Nevertheless they persevered and helped establish Greeley as a permanent colony.

In addition to farming Greeley was also aided by the cattle industry, which was prevalent in the surrounding regions. The cattle became a burden when they began venturing into the colony and ruining the farmers' crops. In order to solve this problem, many colony members advocated building a large fence around the entire community. Although this idea initially met with some opposition, this fence was eventually constructed at a cost of over $20,000.

Although the fence served its purpose in protecting the farmland, residents still faced other problems, in that they relied too heavily on wheat and did not have any other staple crops. This finally changed in 1876 when farmers began planting potatoes. By 1890, 2,000 carloads of potatoes were shipped from Greeley annually, and they were sold throughout much of the United States.

Another important factor in Greeley's development was the establishment of the Colorado State Normal School. This school, which was organized to train teachers for work in public school, opened for classes in 1891. Although it initially only gave degrees in pedagogy, the college has, over the years, expanded significantly, and today it is known as the University of Northern Colorado.

Shortly after the opening of the normal school, Colorado was hit by the Panic of 1893. While the mining towns struggled to survive, residents looked to agriculture to take up some of the slack in Colorado's slumping economy. The farmers around the state, however, had neither the expertise nor the proper financing to establish agriculture as a major industry.

It was not until 1905, when the Great Western Sugar Company was established, that farming finally emerged as a significant factor in the economy. This company, which had a factory in Greeley, began growing sugar beets in many areas of the state. These beets were useful not only for producing sugar, but their pulp could be used to feed cattle. As a result Greeley benefited from both increased farming and a growing cattle industry.

By 1908 Greeley's population had grown to nearly 8,000, and the town had become one of the state's leading farming communities. Although it was occasionally hampered by drought and even grasshopper plagues, the residents proved resilient and the economy forged ahead.

Greeley's rapid growth finally came to an end at the beginning of the Great Depression. Farmers in Greeley were hurt by the falling crop prices and massive dust storms that plagued Colorado and the nation during the 1930s. Many residents struggled to get by, and some were forced to abandon farming all together.

During this time Greeley's economy was aided by the establishment of a new cattle feeding station called the Monfort. Over the years this station has grown significantly, and today it feeds over 700,000 head of cattle per year.

In addition to the Monfort several other large businesses, including State Farm Insurance, Eastman Kodak, and Hewlett Packard, constructed facilities in and around Greeley in the late twentieth century. As a result the economy became much more diversified.

Although a lot has changed in Greeley over the years, it still retains much the same atmosphere that existed in the early days. Many residents still work in the farming industry, and the town retains the same relaxed attitude and warm hospitality that Nathaniel Meeker envisioned when he first conceived of establishing a farming colony over one hundred and thirty years ago.

View of 7th Street in the 1880s shows the Greeley Tribune Building in the right foreground and the Meeker School Building in the left background.

Today most of the historic structures have been replaced by modern buildings.

The Meeker School Building, shown in the 1880s, was completed in 1875 at a cost of $25,000.

CHAPTER VII: THE FRONT RANGE

*T*oday both the school house and the pond in the foreground are gone.

257.   MEEKER AVE.

*V*iew of 8th Street looking across Meeker Ave. (now 8th Ave.) in the 1880s.

*T*he same scene in Greeley in 1997 shows many changes from a century ago.

Chapter VIII
Scenic Colorado

MOUNT OF THE HOLY CROSS: A Shrine

Prior to the arrival of the American settlers in Colorado, the Utes, the Spanish explorers, and the trappers and traders are all thought to have come across a giant cross of snow embedded on the side of a mountain. In later years stories of this cross circulated among the early mining camps. Throughout this time the Cross remaind steeped in myth and legend. To many its existence was as dubious as that of the fabled Seven Cities.

The first written account of the Holy Cross came in 1869 when William H. Brewer and others ascended Grays Peak and saw in the distance a peak "with its cross of pure white, a mile high, suspended against its side."

Following this sighting the Holy Cross began to emerge from obscurity. The real proof for its existence finally came in 1873 when pioneer photographer William Henry Jackson made the arduous trip to the top of Notch Mountain to photograph the Cross.

Jackson's photographs inspired another artist, Thomas Moran, to make the journey to the Mount of the Holy Cross. Moran made several paintings of the Cross using a waterfall in the valley below the mountain to add drama to the foreground.

Yet another artist who brought attention to the Mount of the Holy Cross was the poet Henry Wadsworth Longfellow. In honor of his deceased wife, Longfellow wrote a poem entitled *The Cross of Snow*:

The Cross of Snow

In the long, sleepless watches of the night
A gentle face-the face of one long dead-
Looks at me from the wall, where round its head
The night-lamp casts a halo of pale light.
Here in this room she died; and soul more white

in the Rockies

Never through martyrdom of fire was led to its
Repose; nor can in books be read
The legend of a life more bedight.

There is a mountain in the distant West
That, sun-defying, in its deep ravines
Displays a cross of snow upon its side.
Such is the cross I wear upon my breast
These eighteen years, through all the changing scenes
And seasons, changeless since the day she dies.
(Brown, *Holy Cross*)

The work of Jackson, Moran, and Longfellow brought much publicity to the Mount of the Holy Cross, and it inspired many visitors to make the journey to the summit of Notch Mountain. Many people considered this trip a sacred journey and believed that the mountain lent proof to the existence of a Christian God.

Although many hikers ascended Notch Mountain in the late 1900s and early twentieth century, no organized pilgrimages were made to view the Cross until 1928. In this year the *Denver Post* sponsored the first annual pilgrimage to Notch Mountain. This pilgrimage continued until 1938, drawing as many as 800 people.

In 1929, approximately one year after the first pilgrimage, Herbert Hoover signed a bill creating the Mount of the Holy Cross National Monument. This monument remained in existence until 1950 when it was discontinued due to the mountain's remote location and the gradual erosion of the right arm of the Cross.

Today the Mount of the Holy Cross remains one of the most magnificent and inaccessible scenic wonders in all of Colorado. In a day when roads lead visitors to nearly every corner of the state, this 14,000 foot peak is hidden to all but those willing to make the arduous twelve-mile hike to the summit of Notch Mountain.

The Mount of the Holy Cross was one of the most difficult, but rewarding, peaks to photograph in the 1870s.

CHAPTER VIII: SCENIC COLORADO

Today the Mount of the Holy Cross remains one of the most secluded attractions in the state.

ESTES PARK: From Game Preserve to

In a report for the United States Geographical Survey for 1875, F.V. Hayden wrote of Estes Park:

Not only has nature amply supplied this valley with features of rare beauty and surroundings of admirable grandeur, but it has thus distributed that the eye of an artist may rest with perfect satisfaction on the complete picture presented. (Mills, *Early Estes Park*)

Today this quote seems as appropriate as ever, for the history of Estes Park and the surrounding territory has been shaped largely by the its awe-inspiring scenic beauty.

Prior to the arrival of the frontiersman Estes Park was inhabited by the Arapaho and Cheyenne Indians, who used the area as a hunting and camping ground.The first American to pass through the valley was Stephen H. Long in 1820. Also, Kit Carson is believed to have traveled across Estes Park around 1840. The first permanent white settler was Joel Estes who arrived in 1860.

Although Estes Park now permanently bears his name, Joel Estes and his family lived in the valley for only six years. Their property was then purchased by Griffith Evans, who remained in Estes Park for twenty years.

Another early resident of Estes Park was James Nungent, also known as Rocky Mountain Jim. Rocky Mountain Jim became a folk hero, of sorts, in Estes Park. Numerous stories have been

told of this man including one where he is said to have lost an eye while fighting and killing a bear that had attacked him.

While living in Estes Park Rocky Mountain Jim reportedly had a love affair with an Englishwoman named Isabella Bird. Bird came to Colorado in 1873 and later recounted her experiences in the area in a book entitled *A Lady's Life in the Rocky Mountains.*

One final important figure in the early days of Estes Park was the Earl of Dunraven. Dunraven came hunting in Estes Park in 1869 and 1872 and was so impressed with the area that he attempted to secure 150,000 acres as his personal game reserve. Much of this land, however, was acquired fraudulently and a large controversy ensued.

On one side of this controversy was Griffith Evans who worked to help the Earl secure land; on the other side was Rocky Mountain Jim who strongly opposed the land scheme. This dispute gradually escalated, and one day Griffith Evans is said to have gotten drunk and shot Rocky Mountain Jim. Although he was not killed immediately, Jim did eventually die as a result of the gunshot wound.

Although the early days in Estes Park were certainly eventful, the population remained fairly low until 1875 when many new residents began to arrive. Included amongst these settlers were

Tourist Mecca

Mr. and Mrs. A.Q. MacGregor, who moved into their cabin at the MacGregor Ranch in February of 1875. Mrs. MacGregor went on to become the first postmaster, while A.Q. MacGregor constructed a badly needed toll road between Lyons and Estes Park.

Like Rocky Mountain Jim, Mr. and Mrs. MacGregor opposed the Dunraven land scheme, and in the early 1880s they, along with H.W. Ferguson and W.E. James, forced the Earl to give up the idea of a game reserve. Dunraven eventually ended up with about 8,000 acres, which he used for pasturing cattle for many years. In 1907 this property was purchased by F.O. Stanley and B.D. Sanborn who built the Stanley and Stanley Manor hotels.

With the Earl out of the picture, the door was opened for many new settlers to arrive in the valley. Unlike the mining camps, though, there was not an early population boom in Estes Park. The town matured slowly, but it continued growing throughout the 1890s and into the twentieth century.

Estes Park really began to prosper in 1915, when Enos A. Mills helped pass a bill for the creation of Rocky Mountain National Park. This park attracted visitors from throughout the nation and established Estes Park as a major resort center.

Another factor in the development of Estes Park was the Colorado-Big Thompson Reclamation Project. This project, which was approved by Congress in 1937, was designed to divert water from the Colorado River under the Continental Divide by way of the thirteen-mile-long Alva B. Adams Tunnel.

The first step in this undertaking was the construction of Lake Granby which was used as a storage reservoir. From there the water was pumped into Shadow Mountain Lake and on to Grand Lake where it entered the diversion tunnel.

The tunnel emerged on the eastern side of the Continental Divide at a point along the Wind River approximately five miles southwest of Estes Park. The water then flowed through several power plants, canals, tunnels, and reservoirs, and was eventually distributed to much of the eastern plains.

Since the completion of the Big Thompson Project, Estes Park's economy has remained strong. Today the town continues to benefit from its location next to Rocky Mountain National Park which attracts over 2.5 million visitors per year. Although these visitors will find that Estes Park has grown significantly, they will also find that the land around Estes Park still retains much of the scenic beauty that so impressed F.V. Hayden over a century ago.

◈

*V*iew of Estes Park in the 1870s shows an untarnished landscape. Photo courtesy Colorado Historical Society.

C H A P T E R   VIII: S C E N I C   C O L O R A D O

*T*oday, due to its location next to Rocky Mountain National Park, Estes Park has grown tremendously.

*L*ake St. Mary, shown in the 1870s, is just one of many scenic attractions near Estes Park. Photo courtesy Denver Public Library.

*A*lthough the town of Estes Park has changed dramatically, Lake St. Mary looks much the same as it did a century ago.

LONGS PEAK: 14,255 Feet above Sea Level

At an elevation of 14,255 feet, Longs Peak looms impressively above the town of Estes Park. It is the northernmost "fourteener" in the Rocky Mountains and is the cornerstone of Rocky Mountain National Park.

The first American to view Longs Peak was Zebulon Pike who came in sight of the mountain in 1806. The peak that bears his name, though, lies over 100 miles to the south.

The person after whom the mountain is named was Stephen H. Long who first observed the peak in 1820. Although a few members of Long's party did reach the summit of Pikes Peak, the first attempt to climb Longs Peak did not come until 1864. In this year William N. Byers and three other men made an unsuccessful attempt at the summit. Byers later wrote of this climb:

We are quite sure that no living creature, unless it had wings to fly, was ever upon its summit. We believe we run no risk in predicting that no man ever will be, though it is barely possible that the ascent can be made. (Trimble, *Longs Peak*)

Just four years later Byers would prove himself wrong. In 1868 he, along with John Wesley Powell, W.H. Powell, L.W. Keplinger, Samuel Garman, Ned Farrell, and Jack Sumner, made the first recorded ascent of Longs Peak.

The first woman to reach the summit was probably the famous lecturer Anne E. Dickinson. Dickinson was a guest of F.V. Hayden who climbed the peak in 1871.

The first person to lose her life on the mountain was Miss Carrie J. Welton who died at Keyhole while on her way down from the summit.

The first recorded climb at night was made by H.C. Rogers, and the first climb during winter was made by Enos A. Mills in February of 1903.

Today there are few "firsts" left to be accomplished. Nevertheless thousands of people come each year in a quest to conquer the peak that was once thought unconquerable. Whether or not they succeed, they surely come away with a new respect for the mountain that only those who have attempted the ascent can appreciate.

*L*ongs Peak, shown in the 1870s, is one of Colorado's most famous and historic mountains.
Photo courtesy Denver Public Library.

The same view of Longs Peak in 1998 shows few changes.

View of Longs Peak in the 1870s following a forest fire.

The same view of Longs Peak in 1998 shows a fully-recovered forest.

GARDEN OF THE GODS: A Fit Place for

Prior to the arrival of the white men, the Cheyenne, Arapaho, and Ute Indians all frequented the Garden of the Gods. They were very impressed by the region and invented many stories explaining the creation of the Garden. One such story relates that a great flood once covered all but the top of Pikes Peak. When the waters finally retreated, the carcasses of the animals that had been killed turned into sandstone and rolled down Pikes Peak onto the valley below.

Although the Native Americans' version may have more literary appeal, the real story of the Garden of the Gods begins some 300 million years ago when the Ancestral Rockies deposited sediments near present-day Colorado Springs. While the Ancestral Rockies eroded away, this sediment gradually compacted into sandstone. When the present Rocky Mountains began to form over sixty million years ago, the tectonic forces uplifted and fractured the sandstone. In later years wind and water gradually eroded the sandstone, thus forming the strangely shaped rocks seen today.

The first American to view these rocks was probably Rufus B. Sage who passed through the region in 1843. Sage was very impressed by the Garden, and he later recounted his experiences in the area in his book entitled *Rocky Mountain Life.*

One of the next known visitors to the Garden of the Gods was the trapper Jacob Spaulding. Spaulding stopped in the area during a severe snowstorm in November of 1848. While there he discovered a large cavern inside North Gateway Rock. He and his men, who were headed to California, waited out the winter inside this cavern.

Following Spaulding the next resident in the Garden was John M. Huiskamp. While in the Garden Huiskamp befriended the Ute Indians, and in the spring he joined them in their migration to South Park.

The first group of gold-seekers to visit the Garden of the Gods was the Lawrence Party which arrived on July 8, 1858. While there many of the men carved their names on the red sandstone rocks. Two of these signatures — those of Andrew Wright and William Hartley —

the Gods to Assemble

can still be seen today near the south side of North Gateway Rock.

Approximately one year after the arrival of the Lawrence Party, Rufus Cable and Melancthon Beach founded the town of Colorado City near the Garden of the Gods. While visiting the Garden Cable remarked, "It is a fit place for the Gods to assemble." Ever since then the area has been known as the Garden of the Gods.

While Cable and Beach staked a claim near the Garden of the Gods, the Garden itself was claimed by Wm. Henry Garvin. In the following years many structures were built in the area, and the land changed hands several times. Eventually much of the territory was purchased by Charles Perkins.

Prior to his death in 1907 Perkins instructed that he wanted to give the Garden of the Gods to the city of Colorado Springs. The property was officially turned over to the city in 1909, under the following restrictions:

That the property be forever known as the Garden of the Gods; that no intoxicating liquors be sold or manufactured there; that no buildings be erected there, except those necessary to properly maintain the area as a public park; and that it be forever free to the public. (Gehling, *Man in the Garden of the Gods*)

Approximately two years after the city gained control of the land, an annual festival called the Shan Kive began in the Garden of the Gods. By 1913 it had become a major event with foot races, parades, rodeo events, and the grand masquerade ball. This festival continued until the beginning of World War I in 1917.

Another major annual event at the Garden of the Gods was the Easter Sunrise Service which was first held in 1922. By mid-century this event attracted as many as 25,000 people, and it was broadcast to millions more by way of CBS radio. In later years attendance began to decline and media coverage was suspended.

Although the Garden of the Gods no longer receives national press, thousands of visitors still come to the area each year. Thanks to the generous gift by Charles Perkins, they can enter free of charge and view the same rocks that were admired by the Native Americans, the explorers, and the early settlers alike.

Garden of the Gods, shown in the 1880s, was a popular destination for many of the state's early residents.

Chapter VIII: Scenic Colorado

*T*oday, thanks to the generous gift by Charles Perkins, the Garden of the Gods looks much as it did a century ago.

*V*iew of one of the characteristic sandstone formations in the Garden of the Gods in the 1880s.

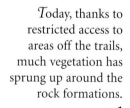

*T*oday, thanks to restricted access to areas off the trails, much vegetation has sprung up around the rock formations.

*V*iew of a rock
formation near
South Gateway
Rock in the
1880s.

*T*he same scene
in the Garden of
the Gods in 1998
shows only
minor changes.

In the 1880s Balanced Rock was a popular tourist attraction.

CHAPTER VIII: SCENIC COLORADO

Although it may appear to be precariously balanced, Balanced Rock has remained standing throughout the twentieth century.

ROYAL GORGE: Site of the World's Highest

Approximately three million years ago the Arkansas River flowed through a flat, open landscape near present-day Canon City. Around this time the land around the river was uplifted, and in order to continue its journey to the Atlantic Ocean, the Arkansas River had to cut straight down through solid granite. It is estimated that the river carved an average of one foot every 2,500 years. Although this may seem insignificant, this erosion has, with time, formed the 1,100-foot deep Royal Gorge.

The first American to view the Royal Gorge was Zebulon Pike in 1806. Pike sent a scouting party into the canyon, but they soon concluded that it was impassible. The party later bypassed the gorge and headed deep into the Rockies. On their return trip they got lost and unknowingly reentered the Royal Gorge. When they reached a point that appeared impassible, the group was forced to climb out a side canyon.

The next person of note to view the Royal Gorge was John Fremont who came through as part of the Corps of Topographical Engineers. Fremont later passed through the area several more times in an unsuccessful attempt to find a suitable route for the transcontinental railroad.

Although it initially appeared impractical to build a railroad through the gorge, the silver discoveries in Leadville in 1878 gave railroad companies the incentive to attempt this engineering feat. In April of 1878 both the Denver & Rio Grande and the Santa Fe Railroad began work on a track through the gorge. Unfortunately there was only room for one set of tracks.

This predicament led to what became known as "The Royal Gorge War." While the crews built tracks during the day, they spent the nights destroying the other company's work. As a result several rock forts were built to protect the lines.

Eventually the whole matter was taken to court, and after six months of legal conflict the D & RG finally relented and gave the Santa Fe Railroad a thirty-year lease on the gorge. Shortly after the Santa Fe assumed control, however, the Denver & Rio Grande accused them of violating the terms of the lease and demanded the return of the railroad. Once again the case went to court, and on June 10, 1879, the courts returned control of the gorge to the Denver & Rio Grande.

Although the D & RG had obtained legal rights to the gorge, the Santa Fe refused to relinquish control, and they hired Bat Masterson to help protect their claim. The D & RG, however, gained the support of Governor A.L. Hunt and forcibly took possession of the Royal Gorge.

Suspension Bridge

In order to prevent any future controversies, the two rival companies finally reached an out-of-court settlement on December 20, 1879. As part of this agreement the Denver & Rio Grande retained control of the gorge, and they paid the Santa Fe Railroad $1.4 million dollars for the work they had already completed. In return the Santa Fe promised not to build in the area for another ten years.

Lost in the controversy between the two rival companies was the impressive engineering feat achieved in the Royal Gorge. The line through the canyon had to be constructed between sheer rock walls that were, in places, as little as thirty feet apart. One section of this track, called the Hanging Bridge, was actually suspended above the river using steel girders anchored to the canyon walls.

As it turned out the railroad was just one of many engineering feats that would be achieved in the Royal Gorge. On June 5, 1929, construction began on a suspension bridge across the canyon. This bridge was supported by 4,200 individual wires, which made up the main suspension cables. The cables, in turn, were supported by large steel towers which were firmly anchored to the canyon rim. When the structure was completed in November of 1929, it hung 1,053

feet above the Arkansas River, thus making it the highest suspension bridge in the world.

Shortly after the completion of the bridge, work began on the Incline Railway. Workers first had to drill and dynamite an opening at the top of the rim wide enough to accommodate the tracks. Steel girders and concrete abutments were laid down the steep slope to serve as a foundation for the trolley. Finally the tracks were laid, and the railway opened on June 14, 1931.

Yet another engineering feat along the Royal Gorge was the Arial Tramway. The first cable used in construction of the tramway was carried across the gorge by a helicopter. The pilot who was given this unenviable task later reported that it was one of the "hairiest" assignments of his life. Once the carry cable was in place, a series of successively heavier cables were strung across the canyon. These cables were then used to support the tramway, which opened on June 14, 1969.

Today while the many engineering feats along the gorge draw thousands of visitors to Canon City each year, the real draw for the tourists remains the Royal Gorge itself. This gorge has existed far longer than the man-made structures and will likely remain long after they're gone.

View of the Royal Gorge during construction of the railroad line through the canyon.

The same scene in 1998 shows several tourists at the bottom of the Incline Railway.

Bibliography

Bancroft, Caroline. *Colorful Colorado.* Denver, Colorado: Sage Books, 1959.

Bancroft, Caroline. *Denver's Lively Past.* Boulder, Colorado: Johnson Publishing Company, 1959.

Bancroft, Caroline. *Glenwood's Early Glamor.* Boulder, Colorado: Johnson Books, 1958.

Bancroft, Caroline. *Lost Gold Mines and Buried Treasure.* Boulder, Colorado: Johnson Books, 1961.

Bancroft, Caroline. *Unique Ghost Towns and Mountain Spots."* Boulder, Colorado: Johnson Publishing Company, 1967.

Bates, Margaret. *A Quick History of Lake City Colorado.* Colorado Springs, Colorado: Little London Press, 1973.

Benham, Jack. *Silverton and Neighboring Ghost Towns.* Ouray, Colorado: Bear Creek Publishing Co., 1977.

The Boulder of Yesterday and Today. Boulder, Colorado: Boulder Chamber of Commerce, 1956.

Brown, Robert L. *Colorado Ghost Towns.* Caldwell, Idaho: The Caxton Printers, Ltd., 1972.

Brown, Robert L. *An Empire of Silver.* Caldwell, Idaho: The Caxton Printers, 1965.

Brown, Robert L. *Ghost Towns of the Colorado Rockies.* Caldwell, Idaho:The Caxton Printers, Ltd., 1982.

Brown, Robert L. *Holy Cross — The Mountain and the City.* Caldwell, Idaho: The Caxton Printers, Ltd., 1970.

Brown, Robert L. *Jeep Trails to Colorado Ghost Towns.* Caldwell, Idaho: The Caxton Printers, Ltd., 1963.

Buchanan, John W. *The Story of Ghost Town Caribou.* Boulder, Colorado: The Boulder Publishing, Inc., 1958.

Bueller, Gladys R. *Colorado's Colorful Characters.* Boulder, Colorado: Pruett Publishing Co., 1981.

Carothers, June E. *Estes Park.* Denver, Colorado: The University of Denver Press, 1951.

Chapman, Joe & Dinah Jo. *The Royal Gorge.* Boulder, Colorado: Johnson Publishing Co., 1965.

Collier, Kathleen, & Ross, Mary. *The Photography of Joseph Collier.* Boulder, Colorado: Pruett Publishing Company, 1983.

Collins, Dabney Otis. *Land of Tall Skies.* Colorado Springs, Colorado: Century One Press, 1977.

Colville, Ruth Marie. *Del Norte, Colorado.* Monte Vista, Colorado: San Luis Valley Publishing Co., 1987.

Crofutt, George A. *Crofutt's Grip-Sack Guide of Colorado — 1885.* Boulder, Colorado: Johnson Books, 1966.

Crum, Sally. *People of the Red Earth.* Santa Fe, New Mexico: Ancient City Press, 1996.

Crutchfield, James A. *It Happened in Colorado.* Helena, Montana: Falcon Press, 1993.

Dallas, Sandra. *Colorado Ghost Towns and Mining Camps.* Norman, Oklahoma: The University of Oklahoma Press, 1985.

Daniels, Bettie Marie, & McConnell, Virginia. *The Springs of Manitou.* Denver, Colorado: Sage Books, 1964.

Dark, Ethel. *History of Jefferson County, Colorado.* Greeley, Colorado: Colorado State College of Education, 1939.

Draper, Benjamin. *Georgetown Pictorial.* Denver, Colorado: Old West Publishing Co., 1964.

Dunning, Harold M. *The History of Estes Park.* (From the books Over Hill and Vale)

Eberhart, Perry. *Guide to the Colorado Ghost Towns and Mining Camps.* Chicago, Illinois: The Swallow Press, Inc., 1969.

Ellis, Richard N. & Smith, Duane A. *Colorado — A History in Photographs.* Niwot, Colorado: University Press of Colorado, 1991.

Fetler, John. *The Pikes Peak People.* Caldwell, Idaho: The Caxton Printers, Ltd., 1966.

Fetter, Richard L. & Suzanne C. *Telluride.* Caldwell, Ohio: The Caxton Printers, Ltd., 1979.

Fetter, Richard. *Frontier Boulder.* Boulder, Colorado: Johnson Publishing Company, 1983.

Foscue, Edwin J. & Quam, Louis O. *Estes Park — Resort in the Rockies.* Dallas, Texas: University Press in Dallas, 1949.

Frink, Maurice. *The Boulder Story.* Boulder, Colorado: Pruett Press Inc., 1965.

From Scratch. Jefferson County, Colorado: Jefferson County Historical Commision, 1985.

Gehling, Richard & Mary Ann. *Man in the Garden of the Gods.* Woodland Park, Colorado: Mountain Automation Corporation, 1991.

Cordillera Press, Inc., *Guide to the Georgetown Silver Plume Historic District.* Cordillera Press, Inc., 1986.

Hafen, Leroy R. *Colorado and its People — Vol. 2.* New York, New York: Lewis Historical Publishing Co. Inc., 1948.

Harris, Ann G. & Tuttle, Esther. *Geology of National Parks.* Dubuque, Iowa: Kendall/Hunt Publishing Company, 1975.

Historic Georgetown. Georgetown, Colorado: The Georgetown Chamber of Commerce.

Historical Walking Tour of Idaho Springs. Idaho Springs, Colorado: The Historical Society of Idaho Springs, 1987.

Hollenback, Frank R. *Central City and Black Hawk, Colorado Then and Now.* Denver, Colorado: Sage Books, 1961.

Jessen, Kenneth. *Eccentric Colorado.* Boulder, Colorado: Pruett Publishing Co., 1985.

Leonard, Stephen J. & Noel, Thomas. *Denver — Mining Camp to Metropolis.* Niwot, Colorado: The University Press of Colorado.

Leyendecker, Listen E. *Georgetown — Colorado's Silver Queen.* Fort Collins, Colorado: Centennial Publications, 1977.

Mangan, Terry Wm. *Colorado on Glass.* Denver, Colorado: Sundance Limited, 1975.

Marsh, Charles S. *People of the Shining Mountains.* Boulder, Colorado:Pruett Publishing Co., 1982.

Mills, Enos A. *Early Estes Park.* Denver, Colorado: Western Arts Publishing Company, 1959.

Norman, Cathleen. *Golden Old & New.* Lakewood, Colorado: Preservation Publishing, 1996.

Olsen, Mary Ann. *The Silverton Story.* Cortez, Colorado: Beaber Printing Co., 1962.

Pearce, Sarah J. & Pfaff, Christine. "*Guide to Historic Central City & Black Hawk.*" Evergreen, Colorado: Cordillera Press, Inc., 1987.

Pearl, Richard M. *America's Mountain.* Colorado Springs, Colorado: Earth Science Publishing Company, 1976.

Pettem, Sylvia. *Boulder — Evolution of a City.* Niwot, Colorado: The University Press of Colorado, 1994.

Rippeteau, Bruce Estes. *A Colorado Book of the Dead.* Denver, Colorado: The Colorado Historical Society, 1979.

Robbins, Sara E. *Jefferson County, Colorado.* Lakewood, Colorado: The Jefferson County Bank, 1962.

Rocky Mountain News, *The Gold Rush.* Denver, Colorado: The Rocky Mountain News, Sept. 29. 1996.

Ryland, Charles S. *Chrysopolis . . . 'The Golden City.* Denver, Colorado: The Denver Westerners, 1960.

Schoolland, J.B. *Boulder Then and Now.* Boulder, Colorado: Johnson Publishing Company, 1982.

Sharp, Verna. *A History of Montezuma, Sts. John, and Argentine.* Summit County Colorado: Summit Historical Society, 1971.

Smith, Barbara. *1870-1970 The First Hundred Years — Greeley, Colorado.* Greeley, Colorado: The Greater Greeley Centennial Commission, Inc., 1970.

Thayer, William M. *Rocky Mountain Railroads of Colorado.* Olympic Valley, California: Outbooks, 1947.

Thompson, Thomas Gray. *Lake City, Colorado.* Oklahoma City, Oklahoma: Metro Press, Inc., 1974.

Trimble, Stephen. *Longs Peak.* Estes Park, Colorado: Rocky Mountain Nature Association, 1984.

Ubbelohde, Carl, Benson, Maxine, & Smith, Duane A. *A Colorado History.* Boulder, Colorado: Pruett Publishing Company, 1982.

Urquhart, Lena M. *Glenwood Springs: Spa in the Mountains.* Boulder, Colorado: Pruett Publishing Company, 1970.

Wagenbach, Lorraine, & Thistlewood, Jo Ann E. *Golden: The 19th Century.* Littleton, Colorado: Habringer House, 1987.

Weber, Rose. *A Quick History of Telluride.* Colorado Springs, Colorado: Colorado Little London Press, 1974.

Wolle, Sibell Muriel. *Stampede to Timberline.* Chicago, Illinois: The Swallow Press Inc., 1974.

Wolle, Sibell Muriel. *Timberline Tailings.* Chicago, Illinois: The Swallow Press Inc., 1977.

Other Sources

Web Sites

http://www.cc.colorado.edu/environment/Courses/CCV/Fiasco.html from Environmental Science Home Page

http://www.azstarnet.com/~dschlos/glenpost/explore/canyon.html from Explore! Glenwood Springs

http://gowest.coalliance.org/ from The Photography Collection, Denver Public Library

http://searchcolorado.com/rifle/stories/022899/fea_0227990026.shtml from SearchColorado.com

Private, unpublished materials

Collier — A History of First Federal Savings and Loan

Collier, Robert. *Robert Collier's Experiences of Fifty Years Ago.*

Collier Ramage, Elsie. *A Few of My Childhood Memories.* April 1938.

Elsie Collier Obituary. January 10, 1914.

Index